ETHICAL ISSUES IN THE 21ST CENTURY

MEDICAID FRAUD CONTROL

INTEGRITY EFFORTS IN SELECTED STATES

ETHICAL ISSUES IN THE 21ST CENTURY

Additional books in this series can be found on Nova's website under the Series tab.

Additional e-books in this series can be found on Nova's website under the e-book tab.

ETHICAL ISSUES IN THE 21ST CENTURY

MEDICAID FRAUD CONTROL INTEGRITY EFFORTS IN SELECTED STATES

KRYSTAL O. HOLTZER
EDITOR

New York

Copyright © 2016 by Nova Science Publishers, Inc.

All rights reserved. No part of this book may be reproduced, stored in a retrieval system or transmitted in any form or by any means: electronic, electrostatic, magnetic, tape, mechanical photocopying, recording or otherwise without the written permission of the Publisher.

We have partnered with Copyright Clearance Center to make it easy for you to obtain permissions to reuse content from this publication. Simply navigate to this publication's page on Nova's website and locate the "Get Permission" button below the title description. This button is linked directly to the title's permission page on copyright.com. Alternatively, you can visit copyright.com and search by title, ISBN, or ISSN.

For further questions about using the service on copyright.com, please contact:
Copyright Clearance Center
Phone: +1-(978) 750-8400   Fax: +1-(978) 750-4470   E-mail: info@copyright.com.

NOTICE TO THE READER

The Publisher has taken reasonable care in the preparation of this book, but makes no expressed or implied warranty of any kind and assumes no responsibility for any errors or omissions. No liability is assumed for incidental or consequential damages in connection with or arising out of information contained in this book. The Publisher shall not be liable for any special, consequential, or exemplary damages resulting, in whole or in part, from the readers' use of, or reliance upon, this material. Any parts of this book based on government reports are so indicated and copyright is claimed for those parts to the extent applicable to compilations of such works.

Independent verification should be sought for any data, advice or recommendations contained in this book. In addition, no responsibility is assumed by the publisher for any injury and/or damage to persons or property arising from any methods, products, instructions, ideas or otherwise contained in this publication.

This publication is designed to provide accurate and authoritative information with regard to the subject matter covered herein. It is sold with the clear understanding that the Publisher is not engaged in rendering legal or any other professional services. If legal or any other expert assistance is required, the services of a competent person should be sought. FROM A DECLARATION OF PARTICIPANTS JOINTLY ADOPTED BY A COMMITTEE OF THE AMERICAN BAR ASSOCIATION AND A COMMITTEE OF PUBLISHERS.

Additional color graphics may be available in the e-book version of this book.

Library of Congress Cataloging-in-Publication Data

ISBN: 978-1-63484-105-4

Published by Nova Science Publishers, Inc. † New York

CONTENTS

Preface		vii
Chapter 1	Medicaid: Additional Actions Needed to Help Improve Provider and Beneficiary Fraud Controls *United States Government Accountability Office*	1
Chapter 2	Medicaid: Additional Reporting May Help CMS Oversee Prescription-Drug Fraud Controls *United States Government Accountability Office*	41
Index		85

PREFACE

Medicaid is a significant expenditure for the federal government and the states, with total federal outlays of $310 billion in fiscal year 2014. The Centers for Medicare & Medicaid Services (CMS) reported an estimated $17.5 billion in potentially improper payments for the Medicaid program in 2014. This book identifies and analyzes indicators of improper or potentially fraudulent payments in fiscal year 2011, and examines the extent to which federal and state oversight policies, controls, and processes are in place to prevent and detect fraud and abuse in determining eligibility.

In: Medicaid Fraud Control
Editor: Krystal O. Holtzer

ISBN: 978-1-63484-105-4
© 2016 Nova Science Publishers, Inc.

Chapter 1

MEDICAID: ADDITIONAL ACTIONS NEEDED TO HELP IMPROVE PROVIDER AND BENEFICIARY FRAUD CONTROLS[*]

United States Government Accountability Office

WHY GAO DID THIS STUDY

Medicaid is a significant expenditure for the federal government and the states, with total federal outlays of $310 billion in fiscal year 2014. CMS reported an estimated $17.5 billion in potentially improper payments for the Medicaid program in 2014.

GAO was asked to review beneficiary and provider enrollment-integrity efforts at selected states. This report (1) identifies and analyzes indicators of improper or potentially fraudulent payments in fiscal year 2011, and (2) examines the extent to which federal and state oversight policies, controls, and processes are in place to prevent and detect fraud and abuse in determining eligibility.

GAO analyzed Medicaid claims paid in fiscal year 2011, the most-recent reliable data available, for four states: Arizona, Florida, Michigan, and New Jersey. These states were chosen because they were among those with the highest Medicaid enrollment; the results are not generalizable to all states.

---

[*] This is an edited, reformatted and augmented version of a United States Government Accountability Office publication, No. GAO-15-313, dated May 2015.

GAO performed data matching with various databases to identify indicators of potential fraud, reviewed CMS and state Medicaid program-integrity policies, and interviewed CMS and state officials performing oversight functions.

WHAT GAO RECOMMENDS

GAO recommends that CMS issue guidance for screening deceased beneficiaries and supply more-complete data for screening Medicaid providers. The agency concurred with both of the recommendations and stated it would provide state-specific guidance to address them.

WHAT GAO FOUND

GAO found thousands of Medicaid beneficiaries and hundreds of providers involved in potential improper or fraudulent payments during fiscal year 2011— the most-recent year for which reliable data were available in four selected states: Arizona, Florida, Michigan, and New Jersey. These states had about 9.2 million beneficiaries and accounted for 13 percent of all fiscal year 2011 Medicaid payments. Specifically:

- About 8,600 beneficiaries had payments made on their behalf concurrently by two or more of GAO's selected states totaling at least $18.3 million.
- The identities of about 200 deceased beneficiaries received about $9.6 million in Medicaid benefits subsequent to the beneficiary's death.
- About 50 providers were excluded from federal health-care programs, including Medicaid, for a variety of reasons that include patient abuse or neglect, fraud, theft, bribery, or tax evasion.

Since 2011, the Centers for Medicare & Medicaid Services (CMS) has taken regulatory steps to make the Medicaid enrollment process more rigorous and data-driven; however, gaps in beneficiary-eligibility verification guidance and data sharing continue to exist. These gaps include the following:

- In October 2013, CMS required states to use electronic data maintained by the federal government in its Data Services Hub (hub) to verify beneficiary eligibility. According to CMS, the hub can verify key application information, including state residency, incarceration status, and immigration status. However, additional guidance from CMS to states might further enhance program-integrity efforts beyond using the hub. Specifically, CMS regulations do not require states to periodically review Medicaid beneficiary files for deceased individuals more frequently than annually, nor specify whether states should consider using the more-comprehensive Social Security Administration Death Master File in conjunction with state-reported death data when doing so. As a result, states may not be able to detect individuals that have moved to and died in other states, or prevent the payment of potentially fraudulent benefits to individuals using these identities.

- In 2011, CMS issued regulations to strengthen Medicaid provider-enrollment screening. For example, CMS now requires states to screen providers and suppliers to ensure they have active licenses in the state where they provide Medicaid services. CMS's regulations also allow states to use Medicare's enrollment database—the Provider Enrollment, Chain and Ownership System (PECOS)—to screen Medicaid providers so that duplication of effort is reduced. In April 2012, CMS gave each state manual access to certain information in PECOS. However, none of the four states GAO interviewed used PECOS to screen all Medicaid providers because of the manual process. In October 2013, CMS began providing interested states access to a monthly file containing basic enrollment information that could be used for automated screening, but CMS has not provided full access to all PECOS information, such as ownership information, that states report are needed to effectively and efficiently process Medicaid provider applications.

ABBREVIATIONS

AHCCCS	Arizona Health Care Cost Containment System
CMRA	Commercial Mail Receiving Agency
CMS	Centers for Medicare & Medicaid Services
DMF	Death Master File
EPLS	Excluded Parties List System
FSMB	Federation of State Medical Boards

GSA	General Services Administration
HHS	Department of Health and Human Services
hub	Data Services Hub
LEIE	List of Excluded Individuals and Entities
MCO	managed-care organization
MMIS	Medicaid Management Information System
MSIS	Medicaid Statistical Information System
OIG	Office of Inspector General
PARIS	Public Assistance Reporting Information System
PECOS	Provider Enrollment, Chain and Ownership System
PPACA	Patient Protection and Affordable Care Act
SAM	System for Award Management
SSA	Social Security Administration
SSN	Social Security number
USPS	United States Postal Service

* * *

May 14, 2015

The Honorable Fred Upton
Chairman
Committee on Energy and Commerce
House of Representatives

The Honorable Tim Murphy
Chairman
Subcommittee on Oversight and Investigations
Committee on Energy and Commerce
House of Representatives

Medicaid, a federal–state health-financing program for low-income and medically needy individuals, is a significant expenditure for the federal government and the states, with total federal outlays of $310 billion in fiscal year 2014. The Centers for Medicare & Medicaid Services (CMS), within the Department of Health and Human Services (HHS), is responsible for broad program oversight, including disbursement of federal matching funds, while states are responsible for the daily administration of their Medicaid programs. CMS also provides guidelines, technical assistance, and periodic assessments of state Medicaid programs. Federal laws require both federal and state entities to protect the Medicaid program from fraud, waste, and abuse. In February 2015, we reported that Medicaid remains at high risk because of concerns about the adequacy of fiscal oversight of the program, including improper payments to Medicaid providers.[1] In fiscal year 2014, CMS reported an estimated improper-payment rate of 6.7 percent, or $17.5 billion, for the Medicaid program, which is an increase over its 2013 estimate of 5.8 percent, or $14.4 billion.[2]

Because of the substantial Medicaid program expenditures and the program's significant estimated improper-payment rate, you asked us to review the program-integrity efforts associated with beneficiary-eligibility determination and provider enrollment in selected states. Specifically, for this review we

1) identified and analyzed indicators, if any, of improper or potentially fraudulent payments to Medicaid beneficiaries and providers; and
2) examined the extent to which federal and state oversight policies, controls, and processes are in place to prevent and detect fraud and abuse in determining eligibility for Medicaid beneficiaries and enrolling providers.

To identify indicators of potentially improper or fraudulent payments to Medicaid beneficiaries and providers, we obtained and analyzed Medicaid claims paid in fiscal year 2011, the most-recent consistently comparable data, for four states: Arizona, Florida, Michigan, and New Jersey. Medicaid payments to these states constituted about 13 percent of all Medicaid payments made during fiscal year 2011. These states were selected primarily because they had reliable data and were among states with the highest Medicaid enrollment. The results of our analysis of these states cannot be generalized to other states. We obtained CMS Medicaid Statistical Information System (MSIS) beneficiary, provider, and other services claims data, as well as state Medicaid Management Information System (MMIS) claims identification data to perform our work.

We performed data matching to identify indicators of potentially improper payments, which includes fraud. These matches sought to identify individuals who may be ineligible to receive Medicaid benefits or providers who should not have received Medicaid payments due to residency, death, or other exclusionary factors. We used the beneficiary files to identify individuals who had payments made on their behalf concurrently by two or more of our selected states. To identify potentially improper payments, we compared the beneficiary and provider identity information shown in the Medicaid claims data to the Social Security Administration's (SSA) full Death Master File (DMF) to determine whether any beneficiaries were deceased.[3] We also compared beneficiaries' identity information from the four selected states to the identity information from SSA official records using the Enumeration Verification System. This comparison helped identify individuals who submitted potentially invalid or inappropriate identity information on their Medicaid beneficiary applications. However, many applications may have inaccuracies due to simple errors such as inaccurate data entry or incomplete sections, making it impossible to determine whether these cases involve potential fraud.

To identify claims that might have been improperly processed and paid by the Medicaid program because the federal government had excluded the corresponding providers from providing services to Medicaid beneficiaries, we compared the Medicaid claims to the exclusion and debarment files from HHS's Office of Inspector General (OIG) and the General Services Administration (GSA). To identify claims that might have been improperly paid to providers with invalid licenses, we compared Medicaid claims data to Federation of State Medical Boards (FSMB) license data for providers that had licenses that were revoked or suspended.

To identify claims that might have been improperly processed and paid by the Medicaid program because either the providers or beneficiaries were incarcerated, we compared the Medicaid claims to data files listing incarcerated individuals from the four selected states. To identify claims that are associated with inaccurate, missing, or invalid addresses, we used the United States Postal Service (USPS) Address Matching System Application Programming Interface.[4] As discussed later in this report, managed-care organizations (MCO) receive a monthly capitated payment.[5] As a result, the Medicaid paid amounts associated with managed care reflect these capitated payments and not the costs of specific services provided to a beneficiary. Consequently, our estimate may understate the actual cost of the Medicaid services provided. All of the states included in our review—Arizona, Florida, Michigan, and New Jersey—had some MCO arrangements in place.

To identify federal and state oversight policies, controls, and processes to prevent and detect fraud and abuse in the enrollment of Medicaid beneficiaries and providers, we reviewed federal statutes, CMS regulations, and state Medicaid policies pertinent to program-integrity structures, met with agency officials, and visited state Medicaid offices that perform oversight functions.

We used federal standards for internal control,[6] GAO's Fraud Prevention Framework,[7] federal statutes and Medicaid eligibility regulations[8] to evaluate these functions.

To determine the reliability of the data used in our analysis, we performed electronic testing to determine the validity of specific data elements in the federal and selected states' databases that we used to perform our work. We also interviewed officials responsible for their respective databases and reviewed documentation related to the databases and literature related to the quality of the data. On the basis of our discussions with agency officials and our own testing, we concluded that the data elements used for this report were sufficiently reliable for our purposes.

We conducted this performance audit from March 2014 to May 2015 in accordance with generally accepted government auditing standards. Those standards require that we plan and perform the audit to obtain sufficient, appropriate evidence to provide a reasonable basis for our audit findings and conclusions based on our audit objectives. We believe that the evidence obtained provides a reasonable basis for our findings and conclusions based on our audit objectives. More details on our objectives, scope, and methodology can be found in appendix I.

BACKGROUND

Medicaid was established in 1965 by Title XIX of the Social Security Act as a joint federal–state program to finance health care for certain low-income, aged, or disabled individuals.[9] Medicaid is an entitlement program, under which the federal government pays its share of expenditures for any necessary, covered service for eligible individuals under each state's federally approved Medicaid plan, as described below. States pay qualified health-care providers for covered services provided to eligible beneficiaries and then seek reimbursement for the federal share of those payments.

Title XIX of the Social Security Act allows flexibility in the states' Medicaid plans. Although the federal government establishes broad federal requirements for the Medicaid program, states can elect to cover a range of optional populations and benefits. Guidelines established by federal statutes, regulations, and policies allow each state some flexibility to (1) broaden eligibility standards; (2) determine the type, amount, duration, and scope of services; (3) set the rate of payment for services; and (4) administer its own program, including processing and monitoring of medical claims and payment of claims. Differences in program design can lead to differences in state programs' vulnerabilities to improper payments and state approaches to protecting the program. States are required to submit plans to CMS to outline their plans to verify Medicaid eligibility factors, including income, residency, age, Social Security numbers (SSN), citizenship, and household composition. With more than 50 distinct state-based programs that are partially federally financed, overseeing Medicaid is a complex challenge for CMS and states.[10]

In order to participate in Medicaid, federal law requires states to cover certain population groups (mandatory-eligibility groups) and gives the states the flexibility to cover other population groups (optional-eligibility groups). States set individual eligibility criteria within federal minimum standards. There are other nonfinancial eligibility criteria that are used in determining Medicaid eligibility. In order to be eligible for Medicaid, individuals need to satisfy federal and state requirements regarding residency, immigration status, and documentation of U.S. citizenship. Beginning in October 2013, states were required to use available electronic data sources to confirm information included on the application, while minimizing the amount of paper documentation that consumers need to provide.

As of March 25, 2011, federal regulations require that certain ordering and referring physicians or other professionals providing services under the state plan or under a waiver of the plan must be enrolled as participating providers, which includes screening the providers upon initial enrollment and when follow-up verification occurs (at least every 5 years). The follow-up verification is referred to as revalidation or reenrollment.[11] As part of the enrollment process, and depending on the provider's risk level, states may be required to collect certain information about the providers' ownership interests and criminal background, search exclusion and debarment lists, and take action to exclude those providers who appear on those lists. When state officials discover potentially fraudulent activity in the enrollment process, states must refer that activity or providers to law-enforcement entities for investigation and possible prosecution.

In May 2014 we reported that states have historically provided Medicaid benefits using a fee-for-service system, in which health-care providers are paid for each service.[12] However, according to CMS, in the past 15 years, states have more frequently implemented a managed-care delivery system for Medicaid benefits. In a managed-care delivery system, beneficiaries obtain some portion of their Medicaid services from an organization under contract with the state, and payments to MCOs are typically made on a predetermined, per person, per month basis. Currently, two-thirds of Medicaid beneficiaries receive some of their services from MCOs, and many states are expanding their use of managed care to additional geographic areas and Medicaid populations.[13] According to HHS, approximately 27 percent, or $74.7 billion, of nationwide federal Medicaid expenditures in fiscal year 2011 (the fiscal year our review focused on) were attributable to Medicaid managed care. States oversee MCOs that provide care to Medicaid beneficiaries through contracts and reporting requirements, which may include identifying improper payments to providers within their plans.

Several federal and state entities are involved in Medicaid program integrity, including CMS and its Center for Program Integrity, HHS OIG, and state Medicaid agencies and law-enforcement divisions. Federal entities typically provide oversight, as well as program and law-enforcement support. CMS oversight of state program-integrity efforts includes providing guidance related to statutory and regulatory requirements, as well as technical assistance on specific program-integrity activities such as audit and overpayments reporting. The Deficit Reduction Act of 2005 increased the federal government's role by establishing an integrity program to support and oversee state program-integrity efforts.[14] CMS collects information from states on their recoveries of overpayments; however, in November 2012 we reported that most states were not fully reporting recoveries and recommended that CMS increase efforts to hold states accountable for reliably reporting program-integrity recoveries to ensure that states are returning the federal share of recovered overpayments.[15] As of April 2014, CMS had implemented this recommendation. According to CMS, the agency provided training to states through the Medicaid Integrity Institute in April 2014. HHS OIG oversees Medicaid program integrity through its audits, investigations, and program evaluations. It is also responsible for enforcing certain civil and administrative health-care fraud laws. States have primary responsibility for reducing, identifying, and recovering improper payments.

INDICATORS OF POTENTIALLY IMPROPER MEDICAID PAYMENTS TO BENEFICIARIES AND PROVIDERS HIGHLIGHT POTENTIAL WEAKNESSES IN SELECTED STATE CONTROLS

Of the approximately 9.2 million beneficiaries in the four states that we examined, thousands of cases from the fiscal year 2011 data analyzed showed indications of potentially improper payments, including fraud, to Medicaid beneficiaries and providers. The numbers on beneficiaries and providers may not reflect the total incidence of potentially improper payments, including fraud, because it was not possible to fully investigate claims that did not have a valid SSN. For example, we were unable to match beneficiaries and providers without valid SSNs to the full DMF, making it difficult to fully investigate such cases for other indicators of improper payments or fraud.

Medicaid Beneficiaries

Table 1. Potential Improper-Payment Indicators Related to Medicaid Beneficiary Identity for Four Selected States during Fiscal Year 2011

Potential improper-payment indicator	Approximate number receiving benefits	Estimate of total Medicaid benefits paid (dollars in millions)
Beneficiaries concurrently receiving benefits paid by two or more states	8,600	$18.3
Deceased beneficiaries	200	9.6
Incarcerated beneficiaries	3,600	4.2

Source: GAO analysis of data provided by the Centers for Medicare & Medicaid Services (CMS); Arizona, Florida, Michigan, and New Jersey state Medicaid programs; the Social Security Administration (SSA); and Arizona, Florida, Michigan, and New Jersey state departments of corrections. | GAO-15-313.

Note: Approximately 9.2 million beneficiaries were examined for this report, with Medicaid payments totaling almost $3.5 billion. The numbers in the columns may not be mutually exclusive, and do not necessarily represent unique beneficiaries. Improper-payment indicators include possible fraud.

- **Beneficiaries concurrently receiving benefits paid by two or more states.** Under federal regulations, beneficiaries are not to have payments made on their behalf by two or more states concurrently.[16] In some instances, a beneficiary may obtain services in a different state, but his or her resident state should pay for the eligible services. We identified about 8,600 beneficiaries that had payments made on their behalf concurrently by two or more of our selected states. Medicaid approved benefits of at least $18.3 million for these beneficiaries in these states.

- **Deceased beneficiaries.** We identified approximately 200 deceased individuals in the four states who appear to have received Medicaid benefits. Specifically, our analysis matching Medicaid data to SSA's full DMF found these individuals were deceased before the Medicaid service was provided. The Medicaid benefits totaled at least $9.6 million in the year we reviewed for these 200 beneficiaries. These benefits could be an indication of improper or potentially fraudulent payments.
- **Incarcerated beneficiaries.** About 3,600 individuals received Medicaid benefits while incarcerated in a state prison facility. We have previously reported that identities of incarcerated individuals being used to obtain benefits can be an indicator of fraud or improper payments. In almost 390 cases totaling nearly $390,000 in payments, the beneficiary supposedly received medical services during the period of incarceration. This suggests possible identity theft since the beneficiary's incarceration would have physically prevented him or her from receiving medical services covered by Medicaid. Medicaid paid about $3.8 million on behalf of the remaining 3,200 individuals in the form of capitated payments. Federal law prohibits states from obtaining federal Medicaid matching funds for health-care services provided to inmates except when inmates are patients in medical institutions.[17] The intent of the federal prohibition is to ensure that federal Medicaid funds do not finance care that is the responsibility of state and local authorities. The claims indicate that the services provided to these 3,600 beneficiaries did not meet the criteria for Medicaid coverage of being inpatient care provided in a medical institution.

Federal law requires states to make Medicaid available to eligible individuals who do not reside in a permanent dwelling or do not have a fixed home or mailing address. Therefore, there are no requirements related to listing actual physical addresses for beneficiary enrollment and eligibility determinations. However, state officials noted that using a virtual address may be a way to conceal total household income and is a potential indicator of fraud. By using a virtual address, state investigators would not be able to visit the residence and confirm the household composition matches the information on the application. Our analysis involving matching Medicaid data to the USPS address-management tool found that at least 4,400 beneficiaries may have been using a virtual address as their residence address.[18]

Specifically, these beneficiaries used a Commercial Mail Receiving Agency (CMRA) address as their residence address.[19] For these beneficiaries, Medicaid paid claims totaling at least $20.5 million.

Another indicator of potentially fraudulent or improper payments on behalf of Medicaid beneficiaries in the four states we reviewed in fiscal year 2011 pertains to questionable or nonexistent SSNs. Applicants provide these numbers to Medicaid to help confirm their identities. Our analysis of state Medicaid information showed that SSNs for about 199,000 beneficiaries, or about 2.2 percent, of the 8.9 million beneficiaries we examined in the four states did not match identity information contained in SSA databases. The benefits paid on behalf of these 199,000 beneficiaries totaled at least $448 million for fiscal year 2011. Over 12,500 of the beneficiaries used an SSN that was never issued by SSA. These approximately 12,500 beneficiaries accounted for at least $76 million in Medicaid benefits.

Applications may have inaccuracies due to simple errors such as inaccurate data entry, making it difficult to determine whether these cases involve improper payments or fraud through data matching alone. In addition, there may be situations where an individual does not have an SSN (for example, a newborn child).

Nonetheless, these applications raise questions because there is no complete electronic record of beneficiaries' identities, which can be an indicator of identity-related fraud. Identity theft and identity fraud are terms used to refer to all types of crime in which someone wrongfully obtains and uses another person's personal data in some way that involves fraud or deception, typically for economic gain.

Medicaid Providers

In addition to beneficiaries, we found hundreds of Medicaid providers who were potentially improperly receiving Medicaid payments. As described below, these cases show indications of certain types of fraud or improper benefits.

Table 2. Potential Improper-Payment Indicators for Medicaid Providers for Four Selected States during Fiscal Year 2011

Potential improper-payment indicator	Approximate Number providing services	Estimate of total Medicaid benefits paid (dollars in millions)
Providers with suspended or revoked licenses in at least one state	90	$2.8
Providers with Commercial Mail Receiving Agency (CMRA) as virtual addresses	220	0.3
Deceased providers	50	0.2
Excluded providers	50	0.1

Source: GAO analysis of data provided by the Centers for Medicare & Medicaid Services (CMS); the Department of Health and Human Services (HHS) Office of Inspector General (OIG); Arizona, Florida, Michigan, and New Jersey state Medicaid programs; the Social Security Administration (SSA); the General Services Administration (GSA); the Federation of State Medical Boards (FSMB); and the United States Postal Service (USPS). | GAO-15-313.

Note: Approximately 881,000 providers were examined for this report with Medicaid payments totaling almost $3.5 billion. The numbers in the columns may not be mutually exclusive, and do not necessarily represent unique providers. Improper-payments indicators include possible fraud.

- **Providers with suspended or revoked medical licenses.** All physicians applying to participate in state Medicaid programs must hold a current, active license in each state in which they practice. During enrollment, states are required to screen out-of-state licenses to confirm the license has not expired and that there are no current limitations on the license. Additionally, states are required to provide CMS with information and access to certain information respecting sanctions taken against health-care practitioners and providers by their own licensing authorities. Using data from the Federation of State Medical Boards (FSMB), we found that approximately 90 medical providers in the four selected states had their medical licenses revoked or suspended in the state in which they received payment from Medicaid during fiscal year 2011. Medicaid approved the associated claims of these cases at a cost of at least $2.8 million.[20]
- **Invalid addresses for providers.** A drop-box or mailbox scheme is a common fraud scheme in which a fraud perpetrator will set up a medical-oriented business and will use a CMRA as his or her official

address. The four states we examined for our review required providers to provide the physical service location of their business when they apply to provide Medicaid services. Our analysis matching Medicaid data to USPS address-management tool data found that at least 220 providers may have inappropriately used a virtual address as their physical service location. Specifically, these providers used a CMRA address as their physical service location. For these providers, Medicaid approved claims of at least $318,000. Additionally, our analysis found nearly 26,600 providers with addresses that did not match any USPS records. These unknown addresses may have errors due to inaccurate data entry or differences in the ages of MMIS and USPS address-management tool data, making it difficult to determine whether these cases involve fraud through data matching alone.

Our analysis also identified 47 providers with foreign addresses as their location of business. These providers had addresses in Canada, China, India, and Saudi Arabia. Our analysis found that 8 of the 47 providers with foreign addresses had been paid over $90,000 in Medicaid claims during fiscal year 2011.[21] In December 2010, CMS released guidance on implementing the Patient Protection and Affordable Care Act (PPACA) provisions prohibiting payments to institutions or entities located outside of the United States. CMS's guidance went into effect on June 1, 2011. Approximately 28 percent of the claims we identified occurred after CMS's guidance went into effect.

- **Deceased providers.** We identified over 50 deceased providers in the four states we examined whose identities received Medicaid payments. Our analysis matching Medicaid eligibility and claims data to SSA's full DMF found these individuals were deceased before the Medicaid service was provided. The Medicaid benefits involved with these deceased providers totaled at least $240,000 for fiscal year 2011. These benefits are an indication of improper or potentially fraudulent payments.
- **Excluded providers.** We found that about 50 providers in the four states we examined had been excluded from federal health-care programs, including Medicaid; these providers were excluded from these programs when they billed for Medicaid services during fiscal year 2011. The selected states paid the claims at a cost of about $60,000. The federal government can exclude health-care providers from participating in the Medicaid program for several reasons.

Excluded providers can be placed on one or both of the following exclusion lists, which state Medicaid officials must check no less frequently than monthly: the List of Excluded Individuals and Entities (LEIE), managed by HHS, and the System for Award Management (SAM), managed by GSA.[22] The LEIE provides information on healthcare providers that are excluded from participation in Medicare, Medicaid, and other federal health-care programs because of criminal convictions related to Medicare or state health programs or other major problems related to health care (e.g., patient abuse or neglect). SAM provides information on individuals or entities that are excluded from participating in any other federal procurement or nonprocurement activity. Federal agencies can place individuals or entities on SAM for a variety of reasons, including fraud, theft, bribery, and tax evasion.

On the basis of our matching of state prison data to Medicaid claims data, we found that 16 providers in the selected states were incarcerated in state prisons at some point in fiscal year 2011. The offenses that led to incarceration included drug possession, drug trafficking, money laundering, racketeering, and murder. We did not identify any Medicaid claims associated with these providers while they were incarcerated.

CMS HAS TAKEN STEPS TO STRENGTHEN CERTAIN MEDICAID ENROLLMENT-SCREENING CONTROLS, BUT GAPS REMAIN

Through regulation, CMS has taken steps since 2011 to make the Medicaid enrollment-verification process more data-driven. The steps may address many of the improper-payment indicators that were found in our 2011 analysis of Medicaid claims; specifically, CMS took regulatory action to enhance beneficiary-screening procedures in 2013 and provider-screening procedures in 2011. However, gaps in guidance and data sharing continue to exist, and additional opportunities for improvements are available for screening beneficiaries and providers.

CMS Issued Regulations Requiring States to Access Additional Data Sources to Verify Medicaid Applicant Information

In response to PPACA, which was enacted in 2010, CMS issued federal regulations in 2013 to establish a more-rigorous approach to verify financial and nonfinancial information needed to determine Medicaid beneficiary eligibility. Specifically, under these regulations, states are required to use electronic data maintained by the federal government to the extent that such information may be useful in verifying eligibility. CMS created a tool called the Data Services Hub (hub) that was implemented in fiscal year 2014 to help verify beneficiary applicant information used to determine eligibility for enrollment in qualified health plans and insurance-affordability programs, including Medicaid. The hub routes to and verifies application information in various external data sources, such as SSA and the Department of Homeland Security. According to CMS, the hub can verify key application information, including household income and size, citizenship, state residency, incarceration status, and immigration status.[23] If properly implemented by CMS, the hub can help mitigate some of the potential improper-payment issues that we identified earlier in our analysis of fiscal year 2011 Medicaid claims including state residencies, deceased beneficiaries, and incarcerated beneficiaries.[24]

Figure 1 shows beneficiary enrollment procedures that states are required to follow beginning in October 2013. Under CMS's regulations, when states receive an application they are to use the hub to verify an individual's eligibility.[25] CMS regulations state that if the information is not available in the hub, or if there is missing information on the application, the state must use other data sources to determine an individual's eligibility.[26] Further, CMS regulations require state Medicaid offices to use all available electronic data resources before contacting an applicant directly.

CMS regulations also say that state Medicaid offices generally must perform checks to verify continued beneficiary eligibility at least once every 12 months unless the individual reports a change or the agency has information to prompt a reassessment of eligibility.[27] These reverifications may include residency or death checks. For residency checks, CMS specifically requires that states use the Public Assistance Reporting Information System (PARIS).[28]

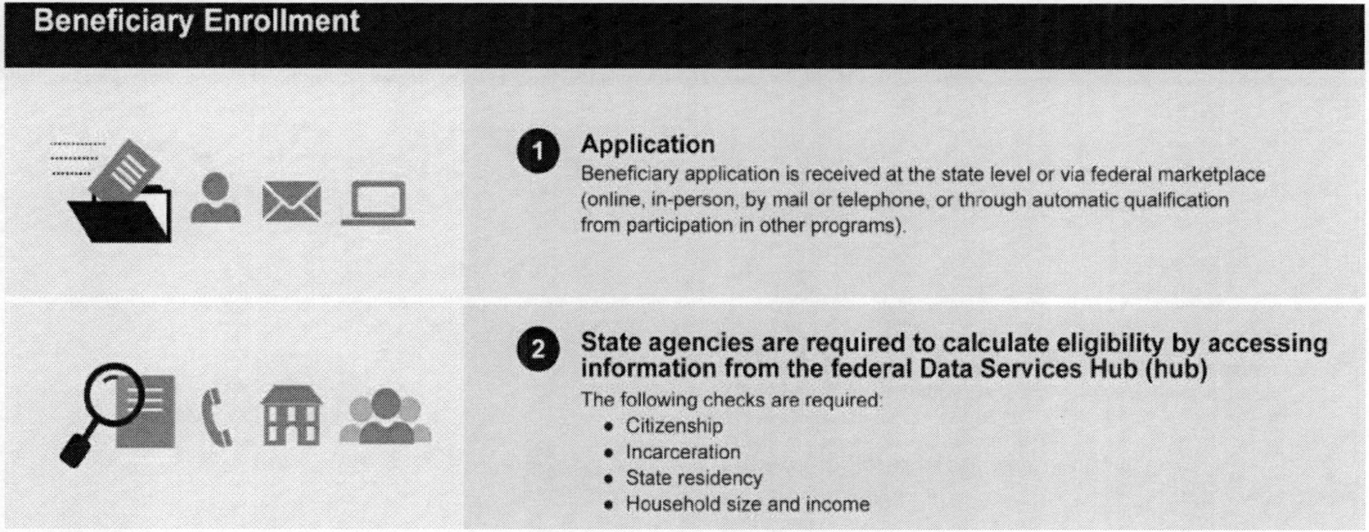

Beneficiary Enrollment

1) Application

Beneficiary application is received at the state level or via federal marketplace (online, in-person, by mail or telephone, or through automatic qualification from participation in other programs).

2) State agencies are required to calculate eligibility by accessing information from the federal Data Services Hub (hub)

The following checks are required:
- Citizenship
- Incarceration
- State residency
- Household size and income

Figure 1. (Continued)

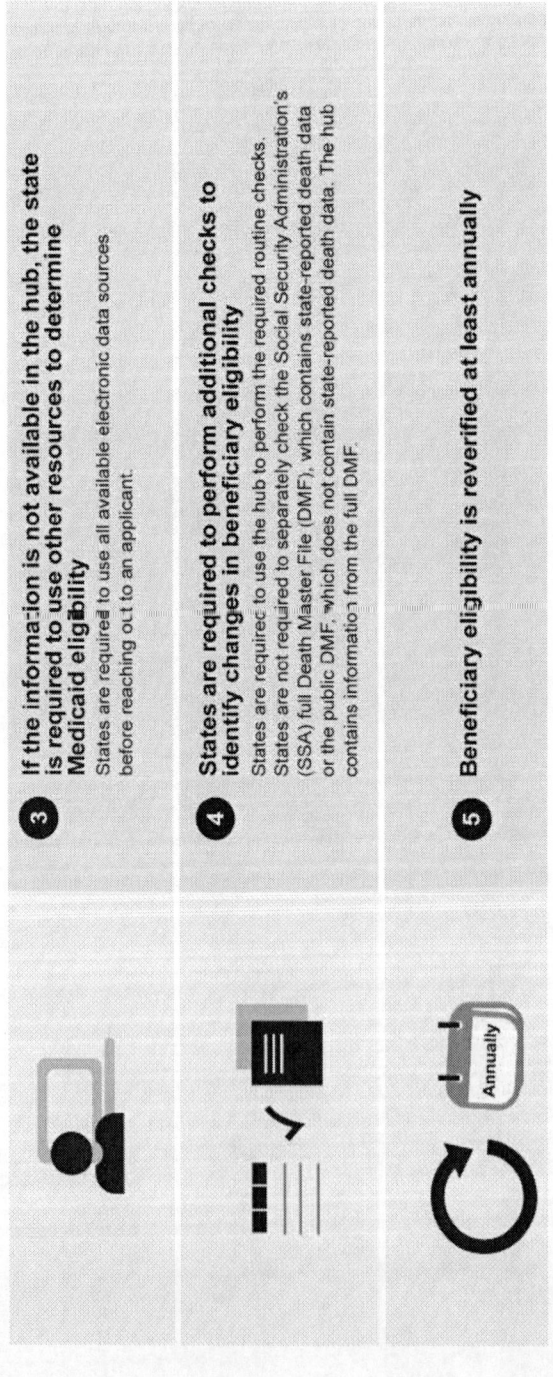

Source: GAO analysis of Centers for Medicare & Medicaid Services (CMS; Medicaid regulations and policies. | GAO-15-313.

Figure 1. Center for Medicare & Medicaid Services (CMS) Beneficiary-Enrollment Requirements for Medicaid under the Patient Protection and Affordable Care Act (PPACA).

This system is used, in part, to identify individuals who are enrolled in Medicaid in more than one state. Thus, by using PARIS, states can identify whether beneficiaries are enrolled in another state and appropriately terminate Medicaid benefits so that payments are not concurrently paid for an individual in two or more states.[29] As discussed earlier and highlighted in table 1, we identified about 8,600 beneficiaries receiving Medicaid benefits in two or more states during fiscal year 2011 in the four states we examined. In July 2014, HHS OIG reported that states' participation in PARIS was limited.[30] HHS OIG recommended that CMS issue guidance to help states comply with the requirement for participating in the PARIS match. CMS agreed with the recommendation. As of January 2015, CMS officials stated that the planned date for implementing the recommendation was March 2015.

In accordance with CMS regulations implementing PPACA, states are required to develop, and update as modified, a Medicaid verification plan describing the verification policies and procedures adopted by the state's Medicaid agency. In February 2013, CMS developed and sent to the states a template on which they were to capture whether they performed certain eligibility-verification steps and the extent to which they used electronic databases to verify the eligibility of Medicaid beneficiaries. According to CMS officials, CMS reviews the states' responses to determine whether each state's verification plan is in accordance with the regulations.

Gaps Remain for Screening Deceased Beneficiaries in Selected States

Medicaid services to individuals are to cease once a beneficiary dies. Under CMS regulations, states are to screen beneficiaries through the hub, which includes a check using the full DMF to determine whether they are deceased, at the time of initial enrollment as well as on at least an annual basis thereafter. Hence, the extent to which the hub identifies deceased individuals in Medicaid is generally limited to about once every year.

To supplement the death verification check from the hub, states may use other electronic resources they have available, such as state vital records, to identify deceased beneficiaries. While officials at the four states we examined said that they periodically check the state vital records to determine whether a potential Medicaid beneficiary has died, the four states did not use the more-comprehensive full DMF to perform this check outside of the initial enrollment or annual revalidation period.[31] As discussed earlier, and highlighted in table 1, we used the full DMF to identify approximately 200 incidents of potential fraud in these four states in fiscal year 2011. Without using information from the full DMF, states can generally only detect deaths within the state's borders and not prevent or detect benefit payments made for individuals who had their deaths recorded in other states' vital records. Additionally, we previously reported the full DMF contained approximately 40 percent more records than the public DMF for deaths reported in 2012 alone.[32] Moreover, in March 2015, we reported that while verifying eligibility using SSA's death data can be an effective tool to help prevent improper payments to deceased individuals or those that use their identities, agencies may not be obtaining accurate data because of weaknesses in how these data are received and managed by SSA.[33]

According to CMS officials, many state Medicaid agencies have long-standing policies of using data matches against both SSA and state vital statistics to identify deceased individuals. SSA has made the full DMF available through the hub for the states' annual redetermination and also has agreements in place to provide death indicators based on the full DMF to states. In commenting on the draft of this report, SSA officials stated that the agency also provides the full DMF to CMS. Thus, states should be able to access this death information directly from CMS, according to SSA. While the federal regulation requires states to check the hub for such items as citizenship and incarceration, CMS officials noted that the federal regulation does not specify how deceased individuals should be identified nor has CMS explored the feasibility of states using the full DMF in the periodic screening for deceased individuals, outside of the initial enrollment or the annual revalidation period. As a result, states may not be able to detect individuals who have moved to and died in other states and prevent payment of potentially fraudulent benefits.

CMS Issued Guidance for Screening Provider Enrollment

PPACA authorized CMS to implement several actions to strengthen provider-enrollment screening. CMS and HHS OIG issued a final rule in February 2011, effective March 2011, to implement many of the new screening procedures. This final rule, if properly implemented, will address some of the issues that we found in our analysis of fiscal year 2011 data, such as screening of excluded providers.

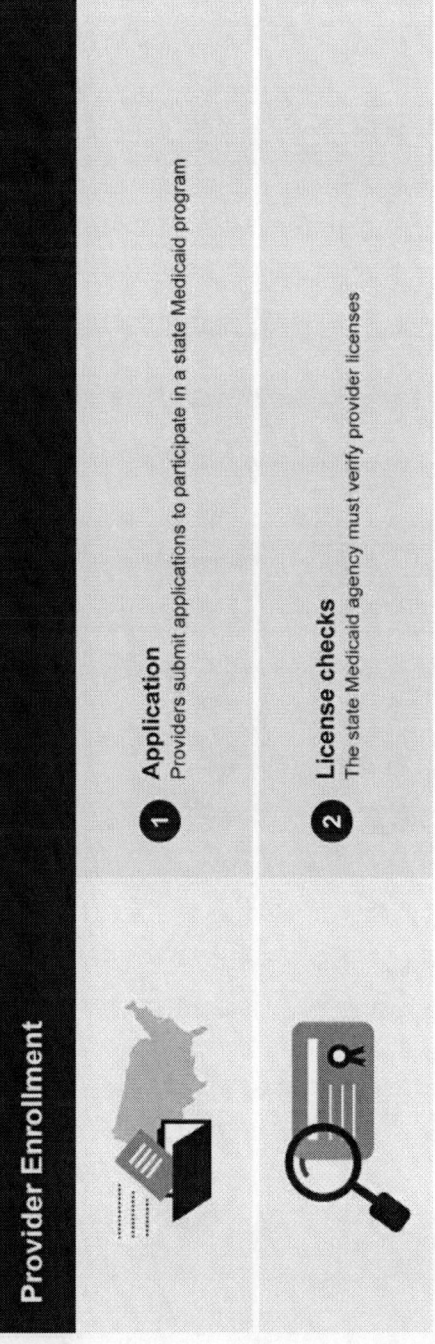

Figure 2. (Continued).

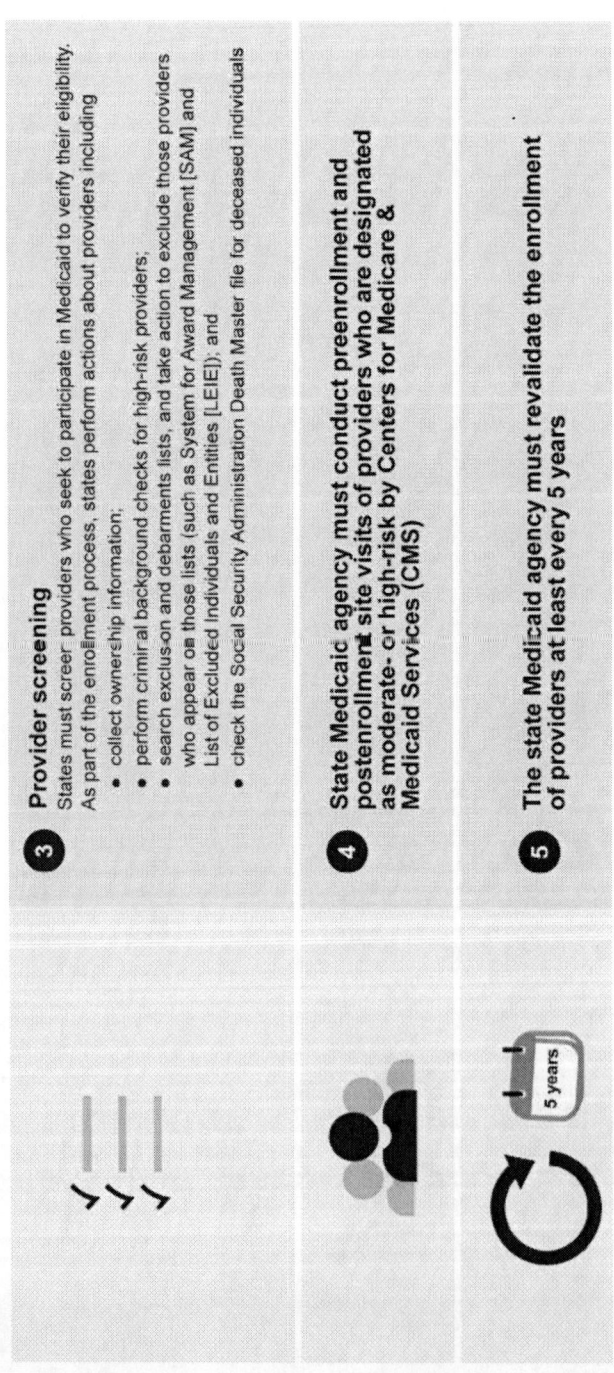

Source: GAO analysis of Centers for Medicare & Medicaid Services (CMS) Medicaid regulations and policies. | GAO-15-313.

Note: According to the Department of Health and Human Services (HHS) 2011 regulation, only those physicians and other professionals receiving payments for services directly from state Medicaid agencies are required to enroll in the state Medicaid program.

Figure 2. Centers for Medicare & Medicaid Services Provider Enrollment Requirements for Medicaid under the Patient Protection and Affordable Care Act (PPACA).

As shown in figure 2, to enroll in Medicaid directly with the state, providers must apply to the state Medicaid office. While PPACA requires that all providers and suppliers be subject to licensure checks, it gave CMS discretion to establish a risk-based application of other screening procedures.[34] As part of the February 2011 regulation, CMS determined that states must continue to verify providers and suppliers using various data sources, such as the full DMF, National Plan and Provider Enumeration System, LEIE, and SAM. According to CMS's risk-based screening, moderate- and high-risk providers and suppliers additionally must undergo unscheduled or unannounced site visits, while high-risk providers and suppliers also will be subject to fingerprint-based criminal-background checks. This requirement may address some of the potentially fraudulent or improper payments highlighted in table 2, including approximately 200 providers with a CMRA or foreign address. Additionally, the regulations require the state Medicaid agency to revalidate providers at least every 5 years. Because the regulation was effective in March 2011, the states are required to complete revalidation for Medicaid providers in their states by March 2016.

We found that the states in our review had different methods for identifying deceased providers.[35] Specifically, according to officials in one state we examined, Arizona, the state uses the public DMF to periodically screen providers.[36] Michigan uses a private-company dataset in monitoring providers for, among other things, deaths; however, the dataset used is not the full DMF but the public DMF, which excludes state-reported death data. New Jersey officials stated that they use a different source of death data—an Internet genealogy website—to check for deceased providers during the application process. According to the genealogy website, it includes deaths from SSA through 2011 and contains updated obituaries from newspapers.

In addition, according to HHS, providers must hold a valid professional license before enrolling in Medicaid. CMS regulations require states to verify licenses in states in which the provider is enrolling and in each of the other states in which the provider purports to be licensed, as well. Two states we examined, Arizona and Michigan, review licenses throughout the country. Arizona uses the National Practitioner Data Bank for license verification. The National Practitioner Data Bank is an HHS nationwide system that is primarily an alert or flagging system intended to facilitate a comprehensive review of the professional credentials of health-care practitioners, health-care entities, providers, and suppliers. The National Practitioner Data Bank contains adverse actions including certain licensure, clinical privileges, and professional-society membership actions, as well as Drug Enforcement Administration controlled-substance registration actions, and exclusions from participation in Medicare, Medicaid, and other federal health-care programs. Michigan, on the other hand, uses a private-company dataset that periodically monitors providers for licenses and licensure actions. New Jersey and Florida both screen the providers within their states, as required. However, neither state uses a nationwide system, such as FSMB or the National Practitioner Data Bank, to validate licenses or determine whether the provider has been sanctioned.[37] Although each state generally had a different process for verification, which is allowable under Medicaid, all four states periodically reviewed licenses to ensure that providers are licensed to practice medicine in their states to meet the CMS requirement.

Federal Regulation on Enrollment Does Not Apply to MCO Providers

According to CMS's February 2011 regulation, ordering and referring providers participating in Medicaid in a risk-based managed-care environment are not required to enroll in Medicaid, and therefore are not subject to screening provisions discussed previously. As explained in its final rule, HHS did not require Medicaid managed-care providers to enroll with Medicaid programs because doing so would have resulted in unequal treatment of managed-care providers under the Medicare program, which does not require managed-care providers to enroll. Although not required, HHS officials stated that they do encourage states to screen managed-care network providers.

In this regard, in May 2014, we reported that neither state nor federal entities are well positioned to identify improper payments made to MCOs, nor are they able to ensure that MCOs are taking appropriate actions to identify, prevent, or discourage improper payments.[38] We stated that improving federal and state efforts to strengthen Medicaid managed-care program integrity takes on greater urgency as states that choose to expand their Medicaid programs under PPACA are likely to do so with managed-care arrangements, and will receive a 100 percent federal match for newly eligible individuals from 2014 through 2016. As we reported in May 2014, unless CMS takes a larger role in holding states accountable, and provides guidance and support to states to ensure adequate program-integrity efforts in Medicaid managed care, the gap between state and federal efforts to monitor managed-care program integrity will leave a growing portion of federal Medicaid dollars vulnerable to improper payments. In the May 2014 report, we recommended that CMS increase its oversight of program-integrity efforts by requiring, in part, that CMS update its guidance on Medicaid managed-care program integrity. In May 2014, HHS agreed with our recommendation, but as of February 2015 had not issued new guidance.

Officials in Arizona, Florida, and Michigan said that their respective states require that all managed-care network providers enroll or register with the state Medicaid agency. We believe this standardization potentially eliminates discrepancies found in states when the credentialing standards for the managed-care network may differ from the state's enrollment processes, and the state relies on contracted MCOs to collect network-provider disclosures, check providers and affiliated parties for exclusions, and oversee other aspects of the provider-enrollment process. Thus, by requiring that all MCO providers be enrolled directly with the states, those three states maintain centralized control over the screening and registration process and may be better positioned to ensure the integrity of their Medicaid programs.

Challenges in Data Sharing Hamper Selected States from More-Efficiently Screening for Provider Enrollment Fraud

We have found that fraud prevention is the most efficient and effective means to minimize fraud, waste, and abuse rather than trying to recover payments once they are made.[39] Thus, controls that prevent potentially fraudulent health-care providers from entering the Medicaid program or submitting claims are the most-important element in an effective fraud-prevention program. Effective fraud-prevention controls require that, where appropriate, organizations enter into data-sharing arrangements with each other to perform validation. System edit checks (i.e., built-in electronic controls) are also crucial in identifying and rejecting potentially fraudulent enrollment applications.[40]

Although CMS has taken steps through its program regulations in providing guidance to states for screening providers, the states we examined reported difficulties in implementing the regulations. One provision in the 2011 HHS regulation allowed states to rely on the results of provider screening by Medicare contractors to determine provider eligibility for Medicaid. According to HHS, this provision would eliminate additional screening and enrollment requirements for Medicaid providers, and also eliminate additional costs and burdens for separate screening for state Medicaid programs.

To administer the provider screening, application fee, and revalidation requirements successfully, as specified in federal regulations,[41] CMS determined that states must have access to Medicare enrollment data to determine whether a provider is currently enrolled in the Medicare program, has been denied enrollment, or is currently enrolling. According to CMS, in April 2012, CMS established a process by which states would have direct access to Medicare's enrollment database—the Provider Enrollment, Chain and Ownership System (PECOS). Each state is given "read only," manual access to PECOS. CMS provided the states access to PECOS in hopes that the states will be able to use these data in minimizing the amount of screening and costs that are associated with providers that are already enrolled in Medicare.

However, according to our discussions with officials in the four selected states, the states are using PECOS to screen a segment of their provider population but none currently utilize PECOS for their entire provider population. Arizona officials stated that they use PECOS in the screening of out-of-state providers. Michigan officials stated that they use PECOS on medium- or high-risk providers to determine whether a site visit is warranted. New Jersey officials stated they use PECOS to confirm an out-of-state provider's Medicare provider status and view the results of the most-recent site-visit inspection. Florida officials said that they do not screen all providers using PECOS. With regard to using PECOS for all Medicaid providers in their screening processes, we determined the following:

- State officials told us that PECOS required manual lookups of individual providers, a task that one state characterized as inefficient and administratively burdensome.[42] According to CMS officials, as of October 2013, CMS began providing all interested states access to a monthly PECOS data-extract file that contains basic Medicare enrollment information; the state officials we interviewed were unaware that they could obtain automated data extracts from PECOS.
- Additionally, state officials from Florida, Michigan, and New Jersey said that they use a limited amount of pertinent information, specifically site-visit information, from PECOS to perform the necessary provider screening. However, there is additional information in PECOS, such as ownership information, that is necessary for state Medicaid agencies to screen providers properly and that is not included in the information that they use. Only Arizona officials stated they are able to utilize PECOS ownership information for providers. According to CMS officials, ownership information on

providers can be obtained through a detailed-level view of PECOS. However, CMS has not made ownership information available to the states through the monthly PECOS data-extract file.

Some state officials noted that full electronic access to all information in the PECOS system would streamline provider-screening efforts, resulting in a more-efficient and more-effective process. Additional CMS guidance to the states on requesting automated information through PECOS and ensuring that such information includes key ownership information could help states improve efficiency of provider screening.

Conclusion

The Medicaid program is a significant expenditure for the federal government and the states, representing over $310 billion in federal outlays in fiscal year 2014. Because of the size and continued expansion of the Medicaid program, it is important that the federal government and the states continue to find ways to prevent and reduce improper payments, including fraud, in the program. Since 2011, CMS has taken steps to strengthen Medicaid beneficiary and provider enrollment-screening controls. As part of this ongoing endeavor, increasing information and data-sharing efforts between the federal government and state Medicaid programs could help enhance efforts to identify improper payments and potentially fraudulent activities. As the federal overseer of the Medicaid program, CMS is well positioned to provide additional guidance on accessing information in federal databases, such as SSA information about deceased individuals and automated information on providers through Medicare's enrollment database—the Provider Enrollment, Chain and Ownership System (PECOS)—that would help identify and prevent benefits and payments to those individuals and providers who are ineligible to participate in Medicaid.

Recommendations for Executive Action

To further improve efforts to limit improper payments, including fraud, in the Medicaid program, we recommend that the Acting Administrator of CMS take the following two actions:

- issue guidance to states to better identify beneficiaries who are deceased; and
- provide guidance to states on the availability of automated information through Medicare's enrollment database—the Provider Enrollment, Chain and Ownership System (PECOS)—and full access to all pertinent PECOS information, such as ownership information, to help screen Medicaid providers more efficiently and effectively.

AGENCY AND THIRD-PARTY COMMENTS AND OUR EVALUATION

We provided a draft copy of this report to HHS, SSA, and state Medicaid program offices for Arizona, Florida, Michigan, and New Jersey. Written comments from HHS, SSA, the Arizona Health Care Cost Containment System (AHCCCS), the Florida Agency for Healthcare Administration, and the Michigan Department of Community Health are summarized below. HHS concurred with our recommendations. SSA did not comment on the findings and recommendations but provided clarifying comments on the full DMF. AHCCCS disagreed with out methodology and provided detailed comments on our findings, as described below. The Florida Agency for Healthcare Administration said it supports our efforts to identify provider and beneficiary fraud. The Michigan Department of Community Health agreed with our findings and supports our recommendations. In an e-mail received on March 24, 2015, the Chief of Investigations of the New Jersey Office of the State Comptroller, Medicaid Fraud Division, did not provide comments on the findings but provided a technical comment, which we incorporated as appropriate. The Florida Department of Children and Families also provided technical comments, which we incorporated as appropriate.

HHS concurred with both of our recommendations. Regarding our first recommendation, to issue guidance to states to better identify beneficiaries who are deceased, HHS stated that it will work with states to determine additional approaches to better identify deceased beneficiaries and continue to provide state-specific technical assistance as needed. In response to our second recommendation, HHS indicated that it will continue to educate states about the availability of PECOS information and how to use that information to help screen Medicaid providers more effectively and efficiently. HHS also outlined steps the agency has taken to address beneficiary and provider eligibility fraud since fiscal year 2011—the time frame for the data used in our study—many of which were mentioned in our report. As described in our report, we used fiscal year 2011 data because it was the most-recent consistently comparable data available.

In its written comments, SSA did not comment on the report's findings and recommendations but provided clarifying information regarding access to the full Death Master File (DMF), which we incorporated as appropriate. Additionally, SSA stated that CMS already has access to the full DMF and can share that information with states to ensure proper payment of Medicaid benefits. We believe that such action by CMS could address our first recommendation.

In its written comments, AHCCCS said that it takes exception to being included in a series of findings that are global in nature and offer no state-specific detail. As we noted in our meetings with all state agencies included in our study, we did not provide state-level detail for two primary reasons. First, because CMS was the audited agency for our work, conducting analysis at the state-level would be outside the scope of our work and would put the focus on a comparison between the states, rather than on CMS oversight. In addition, due to the age and limitations of the data, as noted in the report, we would not be referring specific cases for follow-up. AHCCCS further stated that our report contained misstatements that cannot be attributed to either state. Because AHCCCS did not provide any examples, we cannot address this assertion but stand by the findings and recommendations in our report.

AHCCCS also stated that most of the findings on our report are derived from data sources that are considered unreliable. In our report, we outline the steps we took to assess the reliability of our data and determine that they were sufficiently reliable for performing our work. Additionally, we note the key limitations of the data sources we use for our report and provide the appropriate caveats, as applicable, for the findings from our data analysis. Further, AHCCCS uses several of the same data sources for its eligibility screening as we used in our report. For example, AHCCCS notes that Arizona has found that the SSA death file is unreliable. It further notes that it uses SSA's real-time State Online Query system to obtain date of death information. According to SSA in its written response to the draft report, the source for the State Online Query system data used by Arizona is the SSA DMF.

AHCCCS also states that the findings of our report do not reflect the current eligibility-screening process in Arizona. We acknowledge the limitations stemming from the age of the MSIS data (fiscal year 2011) and the passage of PPACA in 2011. Furthermore, we directly address this limitation in the report where we discuss actions CMS has taken to strengthen certain Medicaid enrollment-screening controls. Specifically, we state that CMS has taken regulatory action since 2011 to enhance beneficiary-screening procedures and provider-screening procedures that may address the improper-payment indicators found in our report. We then discuss the current eligibility-screening process at the federal and state level. We did not make any changes to the report based on these AHCCCS comments, because we believe the essence of the comments was already acknowledged within the report.

AHCCCS also provided comments on specific sections of our analysis, beginning with incarcerated beneficiaries. First, AHCCCS identified reliability and timeliness issues with the SSA incarceration file. This comment is not pertinent to our work, as this file was not a data source used in our analysis. As we note in appendix I, we used each state's department of corrections prisoner database for individuals incarcerated for any period during fiscal year 2011. Second, AHCCCS states that we failed to distinguish whether incarcerated individuals were hospitalized. To the contrary, we note that we reviewed these claims' type of service to determine that none qualified for federal matching funds. Accordingly, this would exclude individuals that were hospitalized.

Regarding our analysis using the USPS address-management tool, AHCCCS incorrectly states that our report assumes that all physical addresses are known to USPS. We do not state this in our report. Specifically, the report notes that federal law requires states to make Medicaid available to eligible individuals who do not reside in a permanent dwelling or do not have a fixed home or mailing address. Therefore, there are no requirements related to listing actual physical addresses for beneficiary enrollment and eligibility determinations. Further, the focus of our analysis was CMRAs used as the residential address, not the validity of all addresses listed on beneficiary applications. As such, the comment from AHCCCS is not supported by the actual content and analyses in our report.

AHCCCS notes that our analysis of provider controls is an extrapolation from the combined set of states' data. This is incorrect. Our report does not extrapolate, or make any population estimates, of provider eligibility fraud. We provided a descriptive analysis of potential improper payments and provider-eligibility fraud based on the data from fiscal year 2011. As stated earlier, we listed the appropriate caveats to our findings to ensure that the results of our analysis were not taken in an inappropriate context, as implied by AHCCCS.

Finally, AHCCCS identified three recommendations that it believes would improve Medicaid program-integrity issues. Specifically AHCCCS stated CMS should

- allow states to use disclosures conducted by Medicare or another state Medicaid program in the enrollment of Medicaid providers,
- allow states to access the federal criminal database to conduct initial and periodic background checks on providers, and
- promote other national initiatives for data sharing on Medicare and provider license verifications.

Seto J. Bagdoyan
Director, Audit Services
Forensic Audits and Investigative Service

APPENDIX I: OBJECTIVES, SCOPE, AND METHODOLOGY

In this report, we (1) identify and analyze indicators of improper or potentially fraudulent payments to Medicaid beneficiaries and providers and (2) examine the extent to which federal and state oversight policies, controls, and processes are in place to prevent and detect fraud and abuse in determining eligibility for Medicaid beneficiaries and enrolling providers.

To identify indicators of improper or potentially fraudulent payments to Medicaid beneficiaries and providers, we obtained and analyzed Medicaid claims paid in fiscal year 2011, the most-recent consistently comparable data, for four states: Arizona, Florida, Michigan, and New Jersey. Medicaid payments to these states constituted about 13 percent of all Medicaid payments made during fiscal year 2011. These four states were selected primarily because they had reliable data and were among states with the highest Medicaid enrollment. [1] The results of our analysis of these states cannot be generalized to other states. We obtained Centers for Medicare & Medicaid Services (CMS) Medicaid Statistical Information System (MSIS) beneficiary, provider, and other services claims data, as well as state Medicaid Management Information System (MMIS) claims identification data to perform our work. Managed-care organizations (MCO) receive a monthly capitated payment. [2] As a result, the Medicaid paid amounts associated with managed care may not be reflected in the state claims that were submitted to CMS for medical services, and hence our estimate is likely understated. All of the states included in our review—Arizona, Florida, Michigan, and New Jersey—had MCO arrangements in place.

To identify beneficiaries that submitted applications with identification information (name, date of birth, and Social Security number [SSN]) that did not match with Social Security Administration (SSA) records, we used the SSA Enumeration Verification System. Specifically, we processed unique beneficiary identification information from the MSIS and MMIS files through the SSA Enumeration Verification System to determine the extent to which SSN information in the MSIS files was accurate. We analyzed the output codes from the SSA Enumeration Verification System to identify unique individuals who had Medicaid application identification information that did not match SSA records. Applications may have inaccuracies due to simple errors such as inaccurate data entry or incomplete sections, making it difficult to determine whether these cases involve fraud through data matching alone. In addition, there may be situations where an individual does not have an SSN (for example, a newborn child). Nonetheless, these applications pose a higher risk of fraud because there is no complete electronic record of beneficiaries' identities.

To identify providers and beneficiaries with identities associated with deceased individuals at the time of their Medicaid services, we matched Medicaid data—MMIS and MSIS—to the SSA complete file of death information from October 2012. We matched records using the SSN and full name of the individual. We then identified unique individuals who had Medicaid claims processed where the date of death in the SSA file occurred before the beginning service date in the Medicaid claims file.

To identify providers and beneficiaries with identities associated with incarcerated individuals at the time of their Medicaid services, we matched our selected states' MMIS data to the states' departments of corrections prisoner databases. Prisoner data included individuals incarcerated for any period during fiscal year 2011. For Arizona, Florida, and New Jersey, we identified provider and beneficiary records for which the Medicaid SSN and names matched that of a person who was incarcerated in fiscal year 2011 in any of the four states. Michigan did not provide SSNs in its incarceration data. For Michigan, we identified provider and beneficiary records for which the Medicaid name and birth day exactly matched that of a person who was incarcerated in fiscal year 2011 in any of the four states. We then identified Medicaid claims associated with the identified individuals by matching to the MSIS data. We compared the beginning service date of the claims to the individual's admittance and release date to identify all claims that occurred while the associated beneficiary or provider identity was incarcerated. Additionally, we reviewed these claims' type of service to determine that none qualified for federal matching funds.

It is not possible to determine from data matching alone whether these matches definitively identify recipients who were deceased or incarcerated without reviewing the facts and circumstances of each case. For example, it is possible that individuals can be erroneously listed in the full Death Master File (DMF). Similarly, a provider or beneficiary may have an SSN, name, and date of birth similar to an individual in state prison records. Alternatively, our matches may also understate the number of deceased or incarcerated individuals receiving assistance because matching would not detect applicants whose identifying information in the Medicaid data differed slightly from their identifying information in other databases.

To identify claims that are associated with missing or invalid addresses, we used the United States Postal Service (USPS) Address Matching System Application Programming Interface (USPS address-management tool). To identify providers and beneficiaries with invalid addresses, we submitted all MMIS data through that USPS address-management tool for fiscal year 2014. The USPS address-management tool provides information such as whether an address is undeliverable, unknown, a Commercial Mail Receiving Agency (CMRA), or contains an invalid city, state, or ZIP code. Additionally, the address-management tool standardized and corrected addresses based on the information submitted. We considered invalid addresses to be unknown/blank, CMRAs, or foreign addresses. To identify providers with CMRAs, we identified all records where the address-management tool identified and confirmed the address with private-mailbox-number information. We conducted further analysis to remove any provider records that were not for the physical service location of their business, such as a billing or correspondence address for a provider. To identify beneficiaries with commercial addresses, we identified all records where the address-management tool identified the residential address as a commercial address with or without private-mailbox-number information. To identify providers and beneficiaries with unknown addresses, we identified all records where the USPS address-management tool identified the address as not found or blank. To identify providers and beneficiaries with foreign addresses, we identified and reviewed all records where the USPS address-management tool identified the address as having an invalid city or state. We removed records that had been corrected by the USPS address-management tool as well as military bases. We then conducted additional analysis to identify MSIS claims associated with both the providers and beneficiaries with invalid addresses. It is not possible to determine through data matching alone whether the identified claims were definitely associated with invalid addresses without reviewing additional information for each claim due to the difference in MMIS and address-management tool data age. For example, it is possible that an address was valid in fiscal year 2011 and was no longer recognized in fiscal year 2014.

To identify Medicaid beneficiaries who received benefits in two or more states concurrently, we identified all beneficiary SSNs that appeared in two or more states' MMIS data in fiscal year 2011. We then found all claims associated with the beneficiary identities. We conducted further analysis to determine the states in which each beneficiary identity appears and the service ranges—first and last date of service—for those states. We defined a concurrent claim as a claim that occurred within the service range of a second state for the same beneficiary identity. For each claim, we compared its date of service to the service ranges for the beneficiary identity to determine whether it was a concurrent claim. It is not possible to definitely say through data matching alone that a beneficiary was improperly receiving Medicaid benefits in two or more states concurrently without looking into further information for each claim and beneficiary. For example, a beneficiary could have been a resident in one state and received services, then changed residency to a second state and received benefits for a brief period, before finally relocating again back to the original state and receiving additional services. In this case, the claims could have been identified as a concurrent claim even if the beneficiary did not receive any services from the original state during his or her relocation period in the second state.

To identify claims that might have been improperly processed and paid by the Medicaid program because the federal government had excluded these providers from providing services to Medicaid beneficiaries, we compared the Medicaid claims to the exclusion and debarment files from the Department of Health and Human Services' (HHS) Office of Inspector General (OIG) and the General Services Administration (GSA). Specifically, we used the HHS List of Excluded Individuals and Entities (LEIE) file from September 2012 and the GSA Excluded Parties List System (EPLS) database extract from October 2011 to perform our match. We matched MMIS and MSIS Medicaid data using SSN and individual name with both the LEIE and the EPLS data extracts. We then identified unique individuals who had Medicaid claims processed where the date of exclusion occurred before the beginning service date in the Medicaid claims file.

To identify claims that might be improperly processed and paid by the Medicaid program because the provider had a revoked or suspended license, we compared Medicaid claims data to the Federation of State Medical Boards (FSMB) Physician Data Center database extract from calendar year 2014. We identified providers with actions that, in some cases, may be prohibited under federal Medicaid regulations that resulted in a suspended or revoked license. We matched these providers with our Medicaid claims data by SSN and provider name. We identified unique individuals who had Medicaid claims processed where the date of license action occurred before the beginning service date in the Medicaid claims file.

To identify federal and state oversight policies, controls, and processes in place to prevent and detect fraud and abuse in determining eligibility for Medicaid beneficiaries and enrolling providers, we reviewed federal statutes, CMS regulations, and state Medicaid policies pertinent to program-integrity structures, met with agency officials, and visited state Medicaid offices that perform oversight functions. We used federal standards for internal control,[3] GAO's Fraud Prevention Framework,[4] federal statutes, and Medicaid eligibility regulations to evaluate these functions.

To determine the reliability of the data used in our analysis, we performed electronic testing to determine the validity of specific data elements in the federal and selected states' databases that we used to perform our work. We also interviewed officials responsible for their respective databases, and reviewed documentation related to the databases and literature related to the quality of the data. On the basis of our discussions with agency officials and our own testing, we concluded that the data elements used for this report were sufficiently reliable for our purposes.

We identified criteria for Medicaid fraud controls by examining federal and state policies, laws, and guidance, including policy memos and manuals. We interviewed officials from CMS and the state governments of Arizona, Florida, Michigan, and New Jersey involved in Medicaid program administration and Medicaid fraud response.

We conducted this performance audit from March 2014 to May 2015 in accordance with generally accepted government auditing standards. Those standards require that we plan and perform the audit to obtain sufficient, appropriate evidence to provide a reasonable basis for our audit findings and conclusions based on our audit objectives. We believe that the evidence obtained provides a reasonable basis for our findings and conclusions based on our audit objectives.

End Notes

[1] GAO has designated Medicaid as a high-risk program since 2003.

[2] An improper payment is defined by statute as any payment that should not have been made or that was made in an incorrect amount (including overpayments and underpayments) under statutory, contractual, administrative, or other legally applicable requirements. Fraud is one type of improper payment and involves an intentional act or representation to deceive with the knowledge that the action or representation could result in gain. Not all improper payments are a result of fraud. Additionally, Office of Management and Budget guidance also instructs agencies to report as improper payments any payments for which insufficient or no documentation was found.

[3] SSA maintains death data—including names, Social Security numbers (SSN), date of birth, and states of death—in the Death Master File (DMF) for approximately 98 million deceased individuals. The more-comprehensive file, which we refer to as the "full DMF," is available to certain eligible entities and includes state-reported death data. A subset of the full DMF, which we call the "public DMF," is available to the public and does not include state-reported death data.

[4] For the purposes of our report, we will refer to this as the USPS address-management tool.

[5] Under managed-care arrangements, states contract with MCOs to deliver care through networks. States typically pay the MCOs a fixed amount each month, called a capitation payment. Approximately 70 percent of Medicaid enrollees are served through managed-care delivery systems, in which providers are paid at a monthly capitation payment rate.

[6] GAO, *Standards for Internal Control in the Federal Government*, GAO/AIMD-00-21.3.1 (Washington, D.C.: November 1999).

[7] GAO, *Individual Disaster Assistance Programs: Framework for Fraud Prevention, Detection, and Prosecution*, GAO-06-954T (Washington, D.C.: July 12, 2006).

[8] Title XIX of the Social Security Act and Title 42, Parts 430–456, of the Code of Federal Regulations.

[9] 42 U.S.C. § 1396a et seq.

[10] In addition to the 50 states, the District of Columbia, Guam, and other U.S. territories have Medicaid programs in place.

[11] 42 C.F.R. §§ 455.410 and 455.414. CMS does not require provider enrollment for ordering or referring physicians in a risk-based managed-care context. See 76 Fed. Reg. 5862, 5904 (Feb. 2, 2011). These provider enrollment requirements were established during the same year as that of the data we used for our analysis.

[12] GAO, *Medicaid Program Integrity: Increased Oversight Needed to Ensure Integrity of Growing Managed Care Expenditures*, GAO-14-341 (Washington, D.C.: May 19, 2014).

[13] There has been a growing trend in Medicaid program administration in which states are transitioning from a fee-for-service model to a managed-care model.

[14] Pub. L. No. 109-171, § 6034, 120 Stat. 4, 74 (2006) (codified at 42 U.S.C. § 1396u-6). In September 2014, the Center for Program Integrity was reorganized to integrate the Medicare and Medicaid program-integrity functions across the Center for Program Integrity, so that all Center for Program Integrity units are focused on both programs. To achieve Medicare–Medicaid integration, the Medicaid Integrity Group was also reorganized and integrated with Medicare staff so that the Medicaid Integrity Group no longer exists as a separate identifiable unit.

[15] GAO, *Medicaid Program Integrity: CMS Should Take Steps to Eliminate Duplication and Improve Efficiency*, GAO-13-50 (Washington, D.C.: Nov. 13, 2012).

[16] Under Medicaid statutes and regulations a state agency must provide Medicaid services to eligible residents of that state. If a resident of one state subsequently establishes residency in another state, the beneficiary's Medicaid eligibility in the previous state should end, subject to appropriate notice and hearing procedures. 42 C.F.R. §§ 431.200- 431.246.

[17] 42 U.S.C. § 1396d(a). For a service to qualify for federal matching funds, an inmate must be admitted as a patient in a medical facility, such as a hospital, for 24 hours or more, and the admitting facility must meet criteria for being a noncorrectional medical facility.

[18] Our analysis found almost 343,000 beneficiaries with missing addresses or addresses that did not match any USPS records. We also identified 10 beneficiaries with foreign addresses (in Australia, Canada, Israel, the Philippines, and Mexico) as their residence address. Medicaid claims associated with these beneficiaries totaled almost $30,000. States must provide Medicaid to eligible residents of the state, including residents who are absent from the state. Regulations do not prohibit beneficiaries with foreign addresses as long as they can otherwise meet state residency requirements, but we did not confirm whether beneficiaries met such requirements in these cases.

[19] A CMRA is a third-party agency that receives and handles mail for a client, such as a United Parcel Service store.

[20] We did not independently verify the final suspension and revocation decisions with the state medical licensing boards.

[21] All 47 providers identified had claims associated with them in the fiscal year 2011 MSIS prescription claims data file, which was not included in this review.

[22] 42 C.F.R. § 455.436(c)(2) requires states to check LEIE and the Excluded Parties List System (EPLS). However, GSA discontinued EPLS in 2012 and moved its content to SAM. In August 2012, CMS officials instructed states to use SAM instead of EPLS to fulfill their regulatory responsibilities.

[23] As discussed earlier and highlighted in table 1, we identified about 3,600 beneficiaries receiving Medicaid benefits while they were incarcerated.

[24] We have ongoing work that is reviewing the effectiveness of the hub in verification of eligibility. We plan to report on the results of this work later in the calendar year.

[25] Under 42 C.F.R. § 435.945(k), subject to approval by the Secretary, states may request and use information from alternate sources, provided that such alternative source or mechanism will reduce the administrative costs and burdens on individuals and states while maximizing accuracy, minimizing delay, meeting applicable requirements relating to the confidentiality, disclosure, maintenance, or use of information, and promoting coordination with other insurance-affordability programs. The data used for our study are from fiscal year 2011, approximately 3 years prior to implementation of the CMS hub requirement.

[26] 42 C.F.R. §§ 435.948–435.956.

[27] 42 C.F.R. § 435.916.

[28] Initiated in 1993, PARIS is a set of computer matches that enables state public-assistance agencies and federal agencies to share information about applicants for and recipients of certain benefits. PARIS allows participating state public-assistance agencies to exchange with other participants the previous quarter's eligibility files for the Temporary Assistance for Needy Families program, Supplemental Nutrition Assistance Program, and Medicaid program. Federal agencies such as the Department of Defense and the Department of Veterans Affairs have likewise signed agreements to participate in PARIS. States can use the PARIS data match to ensure that individuals enrolled in Medicaid or other public-assistance benefits in one state do not receive duplicate benefits in that state Medicaid program or other public-benefit programs in another state.

[29] Florida officials noted that the information in PARIS is dated and use of the system requires a response from another state.

[30] See Department of Health and Human Services, Office of Inspector General, *Public Assistance Reporting Information System: State Participation in the Medicaid Interstate Match Is Limited*, OEI-09-11-00780 (Washington, D.C.: July 2014).

[31] In commenting on a draft of this report, SSA clarified that the agency does not have data-sharing agreements in place with any states for the full DMF, but does provide death indicators derived from the full DMF.

[32] GAO, *Social Security Death Data: Additional Action Needed to Address Data Errors and Federal Agency Access*, GAO-14-46 (Washington, D.C.: Nov. 27, 2013).

[33] GAO, *Improper Payments: Government-Wide Estimates and Use of Death Data to Help Prevent Payments to Deceased Individuals*, GAO-15-482T (Washington, D.C.: Mar. 16, 2015).

[34] CMS and state Medicaid programs are not required to use the FSMB database that we used in our study.

[35] As discussed earlier and highlighted in table 2, we identified about 50 providers that received Medicaid payments during fiscal year 2011 for services rendered after they were deceased.

[36] In its comments on a draft of this report, SSA stated that it does not provide the full DMF to any state Medicaid program.

[37] New Jersey does verify licenses from its neighboring states of Delaware, New York, and Pennsylvania. Additionally, the New Jersey Office of the State Comptroller Medicaid Fraud Division stated that it utilizes a national website to validate licenses and determine whether a provider has been sanctioned, but only for high- and moderate-risk provider-type applications submitted to the state for enrollment into the Medicaid program.

[38] GAO-14-341.

[39] GAO-06-954T.

[40] System edit checks are prepayment or postpayment computerized tests to detect inaccuracies in eligibility, reporting, and payment. For additional discussion of these issues, including associated challenges, please see our overview of the GAO data analytics forum: GAO, *Highlights of a Forum: Data Analytics for Oversight and Law Enforcement*, GAO-13-680SP (Washington, D.C.: July 15, 2013).

[41] 42 C.F.R. §§ 455.410, 455.414, 455.450, and 455.460.

[42] Officials stated that large-scale batch matching is not possible, so they must check each provider in PECOS individually.

End Notes for Appendix I

[1] We vetted 11 states for possible inclusion in our study—Arizona, California, Florida, Illinois, Maryland, Michigan, New Jersey, New York, Ohio, Pennsylvania, and Texas. We selected states based on high Medicaid beneficiary enrollment, geographic diversity, and availability of data. In the selection process, we also considered whether services were paid under fee-for-service or managed-care organizations (MCO), by including states that used these programs in our review. On the basis of our discussions with agency officials and our own testing, we concluded that the data elements from the four selected states used in this report were sufficiently reliable for our purposes.

[2] Under managed-care arrangements, states contract with MCOs to deliver care through networks. States typically pay the MCOs a fixed amount each month, called a capitation payment. Approximately 70 percent of Medicaid enrollees are served through managed-care delivery systems, where providers are paid at a monthly capitation payment rate.

[3] GAO, *Standards for Internal Control in the Federal Government*, GAO/AIMD-00-21.3.1 (Washington, D.C.: November 1999).

[4] GAO, *Individual Disaster Assistance Programs: Framework for Fraud Prevention, Detection, and Prosecution*, GAO-06-954T (Washington, D.C.: July 12, 2006).

In: Medicaid Fraud Control
Editor: Krystal O. Holtzer

ISBN: 978-1-63484-105-4
© 2016 Nova Science Publishers, Inc.

Chapter 2

MEDICAID: ADDITIONAL REPORTING MAY HELP CMS OVERSEE PRESCRIPTION-DRUG FRAUD CONTROLS[*]

United States Government Accountability Office

WHY GAO DID THIS STUDY

Medicaid is a significant expenditure for the federal government and the states, with total federal outlays of $310 billion in fiscal year 2014. CMS reported an estimated $17.5 billion in potentially improper payments for the Medicaid program in 2014.

GAO was asked to review pharmacy-related program-integrity efforts at selected states. Among other reporting objectives, this report (1) identifies and analyzes indicators of potentially fraudulent or abusive prescribing activities in fiscal year 2011, and (2) examines the extent to which federal and state oversight policies, controls, and processes are in place to prevent and detect instances of prescription-drug fraud and abuse.

GAO analyzed Medicaid claims paid in fiscal year 2011, the most-recent reliable data available, for four states: Arizona, Florida, Michigan, and New Jersey. These states were chosen, in part, because they were among those with the highest Medicaid expenditures; the results are not generalizable to all

---

[*] This is an edited, reformatted and augmented version of a United States Government Accountability Office publication, No. GAO-15-390, dated July 2015.

states. GAO performed data matching with various databases to identify indicators of potential fraud, reviewed CMS and state Medicaid program-integrity policies, and interviewed CMS and state officials performing oversight functions.

What GAO Recommends

GAO recommends that CMS require states to report information about specific drug-utilization review controls to determine whether additional guidance is needed. The agency concurred with the recommendation and stated that it will consider requiring states to report on these areas.

What GAO Found

GAO found indicators of potential prescription-medication fraud and abuse among thousands of Medicaid beneficiaries and hundreds of prescribers during fiscal year 2011—the most-recent year for which reliable data were available in four selected states: Arizona, Florida, Michigan, and New Jersey. These states accounted for about 13 percent of all fiscal year 2011 Medicaid payments. Specifically, in these four states, GAO found the following:

- More than 16,000 of the 5.4 million beneficiaries potentially engaged in "doctor shopping," by visiting five or more doctors to receive prescriptions for antipsychotics or respiratory medications valued at about $33 million.
- About 700 beneficiaries received more than a 1-year supply of the same drug in 2011 at a cost to Medicaid of at least $1.6 million. This is an indicator of diversion, which is the redirection of prescription drugs for illegitimate purposes.

As required by federal law, the Medicaid Drug Utilization Review program is a two-phase review process states use to promote safety while also monitoring prescription-drug activity for fraud. Federal law requires each state to report on the operation of its review program, a key monitoring tool that the Centers for Medicare & Medicaid Services (CMS) uses to oversee the review process in states, but GAO identified additional actions that could improve oversight. In the first phase, states use tools and eligibility screening to promote patient safety and avoid abuse before the drugs are dispensed. The second phase involves ongoing and periodic examination of claims data to identify patterns of fraud, abuse, gross overuse, or medically unnecessary care, and implement corrective action when needed.

However, GAO identified two potential controls that are not included in CMS's current reporting requirements:

- **Lock-in programs for noncontrolled substances.** Lock-in programs address doctor shopping by restricting beneficiaries who have abused the Medicaid program to one health-care provider, one pharmacy, or both, for receiving prescriptions. Lock-in programs have typically been used on controlled substances. Expanding lock-in programs that currently focus on controlled substances to restrict abusers of noncontrolled substances, such as the human immunodeficiency virus medications Atripla and Truvada, to a single prescriber or pharmacy may help address potential fraud and abuse.
- **Prohibition of automatic refills.** Pharmacies permitting automatic refills automatically refill prescriptions for certain medications without any customer action. Concerns with pharmacy automatic refill include the potential for stockpiling, continued fill of discontinued medications, and increased cost and waste of prescription medications. Two states GAO reviewed—Florida and Arizona—have prohibited the practice.

CMS does not collect information about lock-in programs for noncontrolled substances or automatic refill prohibitions, but doing so would help the agency determine whether additional guidance is needed.

ABBREVIATIONS

2013 CMS DUR Summary	Medicaid Drug Utilization Review State Comparison Annual Report
AHCA	Florida Agency for Health Care Administration
AHCCCS	Arizona Health Care Cost Containment System
CMS	Centers for Medicare & Medicaid Services

DMAHS	State of New Jersey, Department of Human Services, Division of Medical Assistance and Health Services
DMF	Death Master File
DUR	Drug Utilization Review
FFS	fee-for-service
GSA	General Services Administration
HHS	Department of Health and Human Services
HIV	human immunodeficiency virus
MCO	managed-care organization
MMIS	Medicaid Management Information System
MSIS	Medicaid Statistical Information System
OIG	Office of Inspector General
SAM	System for Award Management
SSA	Social Security Administration
SSN	Social Security number
T-MSIS	Transformed Medicaid Statistical Information System

* * *

July 8, 2015

Congressional Requesters

Established in 1965 by Title XIX of the Social Security Act, Medicaid is a joint federal–state program that finances health care for low-income and medically needy individuals. The Centers for Medicare & Medicaid Services (CMS), within the Department of Health and Human Services (HHS), is responsible for overseeing the Medicaid program, including disbursing federal matching funds, and provides guidance, technical assistance, and periodic assessments of state Medicaid programs. Federal laws prescribe responsibility for both federal and state entities to protect the Medicaid program from fraud, waste, and abuse. Specifically, federal law requires CMS to issue regulations to improve Medicaid program integrity, with which state Medicaid programs must comply.

Medicaid is a significant expenditure for the federal government and the states, with total federal outlays of $310 billion in fiscal year 2014. In February 2015, we reported that Medicaid remains at high risk because of concerns about the adequacy of fiscal oversight of the program, including improper payments to Medicaid providers.[1] In fiscal year 2014, CMS reported an estimated improper payment rate of 6.7 percent, or $17.5 billion for the Medicaid program, which is an increase over its 2013 estimate of 5.8 percent, or $14.4 billion.[2]

While most improper payments are not related to fraud, and the full extent to which fraud, waste, and abuse related to prescription drugs affects Medicaid is unknown, we have previously identified potentially fraudulent or abusive practices in CMS's health-care programs.[3] For example, in September 2009, we found tens of thousands of potential "doctor shoppers" of controlled substances in Medicaid.[4] Doctor shopping is a beneficiary fraud scheme in which patients visit several doctors and pharmacies, receiving more drugs than any single physician would have prescribed. Additionally, in September 2011, we reported on indications of doctor shopping in the Medicare Part D program, which provides voluntary, outpatient prescription-drug coverage for eligible individuals 65 years and older and eligible individuals with disabilities.[5] As part of that work, we found that about 170,000 Medicare beneficiaries received prescriptions from five or more medical practitioners for frequently abused controlled substances. In both of those reports we made recommendations that CMS improve efforts to address doctor shopping. CMS agreed with our recommendations and implemented them. In May 2015, we issued a report on our work associated with Medicaid beneficiary and provider fraud.

Because of the substantial amount of funds that are expended in the Medicaid program and our prior work detailing potential fraudulent or abusive practices, you asked us to review any pharmacy-related program-integrity efforts at selected states. Specifically, for this review we

1) evaluated the reliability of Medicaid data from CMS and selected states for the purpose of identifying indicators of potential fraud or abuse;
2) identified and analyzed indicators, if any, of potentially fraudulent or abusive activities related to prescription drugs in Medicaid; and
3) examined the extent to which federal and selected state oversight policies, controls, and processes are designed to prevent and detect instances of prescription-drug fraud in Medicaid.

To evaluate the reliability of Medicaid data from CMS and state Medicaid programs for our selected states that could be used to identify indicators of potential fraud or abuse, we took several steps. We vetted 11 states for possible inclusion in our study.[6] We selected states based on high Medicaid beneficiary enrollment, geographic diversity, and availability of data. In the selection process, we also considered whether drugs were paid under fee-for-service (FFS) or managed care, by including states that included these program types in our review. We performed electronic testing to determine the validity of specific data elements in the federal and selected states' databases that we used to perform our work. We also reviewed related documentation, including data layouts and agency reports. Specifically, we used a January 2013 *Mathematica Policy Report* that details Medicaid Statistical Information System (MSIS) state data characteristics and anomalies to further vet states selected for our audit work.[7] We also used published GAO and HHS Office of Inspector General (OIG) reports that detailed the limitations of the MSIS data we used for our study.[8] Additionally, we interviewed officials responsible for their respective databases to discuss data-reliability considerations, and reviewed prior work related to the quality of the MSIS data used for our study.[9] On the basis of our discussions with agency officials and our own testing, we concluded that the data elements from four states—Arizona, Florida, Michigan, and New Jersey—used for this report were sufficiently reliable for the purpose of identifying indicators of potential fraud or abuse. However, in assessing the reliability of the data, we observed reportable shortcomings such as issues with timeliness, completeness, and accuracy in the data that may affect Medicaid administrators' ability to effectively oversee their program. However, the results of the data-reliability evaluation only apply to the states we selected for fiscal year 2011 and cannot be generalized to other states or periods. We discuss these shortcomings in greater detail later in this report.

To identify indicators of potentially fraudulent or abusive activities related to prescription drugs in Medicaid, we obtained and analyzed Medicaid claims paid in fiscal year 2011, the most-recent period from which we could draw reliable data, for four states: Arizona, Florida, Michigan, and New Jersey. Medicaid payments to these states constituted about 13 percent of all Medicaid payments made during fiscal year 2011. These states were selected primarily because they had consistently comparable and reliable data and were among the states with the highest Medicaid expenditures. The results of our analysis of these states are not generalizable to other states.

We obtained MSIS beneficiary, provider, prescription-drug, and other services claims data, as well as state Medicaid Management Information Systems (MMIS) crosswalk data (with personal identifiers) to perform our work.[10] The crosswalk data we used contained specific identifying information on prescribers, pharmacies, and beneficiaries that were not collected in the MSIS data, such as name and address.

We reviewed literature related to health-care fraud, including reports discussing fraud, waste, and abuse related to prescription drugs. We interviewed federal, state, and private-sector auditors, program administrators, and other relevant officials that had published work that investigated or researched prescription-drug fraud. On the basis of this research, we identified areas at greater risk of fraud and abuse such as drugs at high risk for diversion and types of prescribing patterns that warranted additional review. We used this information to develop our analytic approach to identify indicators of potential fraud and abuse related to prescription drugs in Medicaid. To identify potential overuse, we reviewed beneficiaries who received more than a 480-day supply of the same medication in a single year based on the national drug code. To identify potential doctor-shopping activities, we examined beneficiaries who received prescriptions for drugs within one of two therapeutic classes of drugs from five or more prescribers. We focused on beneficiaries who received prescriptions for antipsychotics or respiratory medications from five or more different prescribers over the course of 1 year. We selected medications in these therapeutic classes because they had a large number of individuals who received drugs from five or more prescribers relative to other classes of noncontrolled substances we considered, have a known diversion risk, and are relatively expensive.[11] We selected the five-or-more prescribers threshold based on our review of drug diversion literature and prior GAO work. We also looked for prescribers and pharmacies with a high proportion of prescribing or dispensing activities for brand-name drugs (versus generics) compared to the average activity of other prescribers and pharmacies[12] and we looked for pharmacies without any adjusted or voided claims.[13] To identify potentially unnecessary prescription-drug activities, we reviewed claims paid on behalf of beneficiaries who received human immunodeficiency virus (HIV) and diabetes medications despite having no HIV or diabetes-related indicators related to such ailments in their fiscal year 2011 Medicaid outpatient claims listed in the MSIS "other services" file.[14]

We also matched the Medicaid data to other external sources to identify potential fraud and improper payments. These matches sought to identify individuals who may be ineligible to receive Medicaid benefits or providers who should not have received Medicaid payments due to residency, death, or other exclusionary factors. We used the beneficiary files to identify individuals who had payments made on their behalf concurrently by two or more of our selected states. We compared the beneficiary and prescriber identity information shown in the Medicaid claims data to the Social Security Administration's (SSA) complete file of death information to determine whether any individuals were reportedly deceased when they purportedly prescribed, dispensed, or received prescription drugs from Medicaid. To identify prescription-drug claims that might have been improperly processed and paid by the Medicaid program because either the prescribers or beneficiaries were incarcerated, we compared the Medicaid claims to data files listing incarcerated individuals from the four selected states. To identify claims that might have been improperly processed and paid by the Medicaid program because the federal government had banned the corresponding prescribers from providing services to Medicaid beneficiaries, we compared the Medicaid claims to the exclusion and debarment files from the HHS OIG and the General Services Administration (GSA). We compared files from the different states to identify beneficiaries who received concurrent benefits from multiple states.

To determine the extent to which federal and state oversight policies, controls, and processes are designed to prevent and detect indicators of prescription-drug fraud in Medicaid, we reviewed CMS and state Medicaid policies pertinent to program integrity over pharmaceuticals, met with CMS officials, and visited state Medicaid offices that perform oversight functions for the four states we selected. We used federal standards for internal control,[15] GAO's Fraud Prevention Framework,[16] and Medicaid statutes and regulations addressing the administration of pharmacy benefits to evaluate these functions.

To determine the reliability of the data used in our analysis, we performed electronic testing to determine the validity of specific data elements in the federal and selected states' databases that we used to perform our work. We also interviewed officials responsible for their respective databases and reviewed documentation related to the databases and literature related to the quality of the data. On the basis of our discussions with agency officials and our own testing, we concluded that the data elements used for this report were sufficiently reliable for our purposes.

We conducted this performance audit from March 2014 to July 2015 in accordance with generally accepted government auditing standards. Those standards require that we plan and perform the audit to obtain sufficient, appropriate evidence to provide a reasonable basis for our audit findings and conclusions based on our audit objectives. We believe that the evidence obtained provides a reasonable basis for our findings and conclusions based on our audit objectives. More details on our objectives, scope, and methodology can be found in appendix I.

BACKGROUND

Medicaid Prescription-Drug Programs

State Medicaid programs do not directly purchase prescription drugs but instead reimburse pharmacies for covered prescription drugs dispensed to Medicaid beneficiaries. States operate their Medicaid programs by paying qualified health-care providers (including prescribers and pharmacies) for a range of covered services provided to eligible beneficiaries and then seeking reimbursement for the federal share of those payments. States may directly pay health-care providers for services rendered using a FFS delivery system or may delegate these responsibilities to managed-care organizations (MCO). Under managed-care arrangements, states contract with MCOs to deliver care through networks. States typically pay the MCOs a fixed amount each month, called a capitation payment. All four of the states included in our review—Arizona, Florida, Michigan, and New Jersey—had MCO arrangements in place.

Although the federal government establishes broad requirements, each state has flexibility in managing its Medicaid program. Guidelines established by federal statutes, regulations, and policies allow each state to (1) broaden its eligibility standards; (2) determine the type, amount, duration, and scope of services; (3) set the rate of payment for services; and (4) administer its own program, including enrollment of providers and beneficiaries, processing and monitoring of medical claims, payment of claims, and maintenance of fraud-prevention programs. CMS is responsible for administering legislation and regulations affecting the Medicaid program. CMS also provides guidelines, technical assistance, and periodic assessments of state Medicaid programs.

The federal government requires coverage for certain mandatory services under Medicaid, but states may decide to include other optional services as well. Some of the largest and most commonly included services include nursing facilities, home and community-based care, and hospital inpatient care. Although pharmacy coverage is an optional service under federal Medicaid law, all 50 states currently provide coverage for prescription drugs. States may pay for drugs dispensed through MCOs using either the "carve-in" or the "carve-out" approach. To use the carve-in approach, states include payment for the drugs dispensed to beneficiaries in the MCOs' fixed monthly payment amounts. In the carve-out approach, states exclude payment for the drugs dispensed to beneficiaries from the MCOs' fixed monthly payment amounts and instead pay for these drugs using the traditional FFS system. States may also use a combination of carve-out and carve-in approaches.

Medicaid Data Collection and Reporting

The Medicaid prescription-drug programs, such as the Drug Utilization Reviews (DUR), include the management, development, and administration of systems and the data collection necessary to operate them. As part of data-collection efforts, states are mandated to report FFS claims and individual encounter data for managed-care enrollees to CMS. MSIS is the mechanism by which CMS requires states to report these data on a quarterly basis, although delays in reporting data occur.[17] The database is used for analytical research, program integrity, planning, budgeting, and policy analyses associated with Medicaid.

Medicaid Pharmacy Fraud

Federal law prohibits Medicaid providers and beneficiaries from taking certain actions related to billing for or receiving Medicaid services. For example, the Federal False Claims Act makes it illegal to submit false claims to Medicare, Medicaid, and other government health-care programs for payment.[18] Violation of these or other relevant laws and regulations may constitute fraud. We and other federal oversight entities have recently issued a number of reports related to fraud and other types of improper payments in CMS's health-care programs, including Medicaid.[19] For example, in May 2014 we reported that neither state nor federal Medicaid entities were well positioned to identify improper payments made to MCOs due to a gap in state and federal efforts to ensure Medicaid managed-care program integrity. A report released by the HHS OIG in August 2014 found over 1,500 Medicare beneficiaries who had questionable utilization patterns for HIV drugs, including beneficiaries who had no indication of HIV in their Medicare histories, received an excessive dose or supply of HIV drugs, or received HIV drugs from a high number of pharmacies or prescribers. In October 2014, we reported on 23 practices for addressing prescription-drug fraud, waste, and abuse in Medicare developed from a detailed literature review as well as interviews with relevant stakeholders.[20]

RELIABILITY ISSUES LIMIT USEFULNESS OF MEDICAID DATA FOR IDENTIFYING INDICATORS OF POTENTIAL FRAUD AND ABUSE

According to CMS guidance to state Medicaid directors, programs with the size and scope of Medicaid require robust, timely, and accurate data to identify potential fraud or waste. However, CMS's MSIS data continue to have limited usefulness for identifying fraud, waste, and abuse due to issues with accuracy, completeness, and timeliness.[21]

We analyzed 11 states to possibly include in our study, but had to exclude data from four states—California, Maryland, Ohio, and Pennsylvania—due to fiscal year 2011 data-availability and quality issues.[22]

- In California, officials expressed concerns regarding the reliability of their data due to issues of reporting from the health plans and data conversions to other systems. Officials also had concerns about the ability to identify prescribing providers in the MCO data.
- The January 2013 Mathematica Policy Research report noted that for Maryland fiscal year 2011 MSIS data, National Provider Identifier (a unique identifier for Medicaid providers) and physician-specialty information were missing on managed-care prescription transactions.
- Similarly, the January 2013 Mathematica Policy Research report identified that Ohio MSIS data were missing provider-identifying information and prescription-drug and pharmacy information.
- The January 2013 Mathematica Policy Research report identified that Pennsylvania had not reported any data related to managed-care encounters through at least the fourth quarter of fiscal year 2011, even though the majority of the state's Medicaid-eligible population was enrolled in comprehensive managed care.

Although the MSIS data from Arizona, Florida, Michigan, and New Jersey were sufficiently reliable for the purpose of identifying indicators of potential fraud or abuse, we identified issues with their timeliness and completeness. For example, the most-recent validated data available from

CMS for Arizona, Florida, Michigan, and New Jersey were more than 3 years past the date when they should have been validated.[23] The fiscal year 2011 claim files were the most-current claim files contained in the MSIS system.[24] In addition, about 20 million (26 percent) of the records included filler data (e.g., 01-01-0001) in the prescribed date fields. While the data help identify potential vulnerabilities to Medicaid prescription-drug fraud, waste, and abuse, they are not sufficiently timely to enable investigation of specific transactions. These problems with the MSIS data used for this review are consistent with concerns raised in previous GAO and HHS OIG reports.

In October 2012, we reported that MSIS data were not timely because of late state submissions and the time it takes CMS to review and validate data.[25] In that report we found that 37 states were late with their quarterly data by six quarters in July 2012. We further reported that even though CMS requires states to submit MSIS data within 45 days, states' reporting of MSIS data and the subsequent validation process can be up to 3 years late. In interviews for this review, both CMS and state Medicaid officials agreed that this validation process can be lengthy. For example, CMS officials may identify a data-quality issue during the validation process in which they analyze the data and ensure that errors do not exceed a predetermined threshold. If the threshold is exceeded, CMS will then request the state to resubmit corrected data, which can take several additional months, according to both CMS and state Medicaid officials.

In addition, we reported in June 2012 that MSIS-based audits were hampered by deficiencies in the data, and noted that CMS had initiatives to transition into a new system called the Transformed Medicaid Statistical Information System (T-MSIS).[26] According to August 2013 CMS guidance to state Medicaid directors, T-MSIS is intended to modernize and enhance the way states will submit operational data about beneficiaries, providers, claims, and encounters and will be the foundation of a robust state and national analytic data infrastructure. Additionally, in the August 2013 CMS guidance to state Medicaid directors, CMS stated that this change will enhance the agency's ability to observe trends or patterns indicating potential fraud, waste, and abuse in the state Medicaid programs to prevent or mitigate the effect of these activities.

States may also have enhanced capabilities to counter fraud, waste, and abuse capabilities. The guidance also indicates CMS and the states will be able to analyze the data submitted by the states along with other information in the CMS data repositories, including Medicare data, enhancing abilities to better identify potential anomalies for further investigation.

CMS officials stated that they will not begin to analyze the benefits derived from T-MSIS until the transition reaches the point where data for at least half of the Medicaid population in the United States are included in T-MSIS.

Our review of prior HHS OIG work and our discussions with officials from our four selected states indicate there may be challenges related to implementing the T-MSIS initiative. In January 2013, the HHS OIG analyzed results of the early implementation of T-MSIS among 12 volunteer states to refine and enhance the MSIS data set and modernize the ongoing submission and quality-review process for the data set.[27] The HHS OIG found that, as of January 2013, CMS and 12 volunteer states had made some progress in implementing T-MSIS; however, early T-MSIS implementation outcomes raised questions about the completeness and accuracy of T-MSIS data upon national implementation.

According to the HHS OIG report, none of the 12 volunteer states could make all T-MSIS data elements available. Both CMS and the 12 states expressed concerns about the accuracy of the data they could provide upon implementation. The HHS OIG recommended that CMS ensure that states report complete, accurate, and timely information to T-MSIS to support effective oversight. According to the Fiscal Year 2016 HHS OIG Justification of Estimates for Appropriations Committees, this recommendation remains a priority unimplemented recommendation.[28]

CMS began implementing T-MSIS with states on a rolling basis in July 2014 and is working towards full implementation in 2015. Specifically, CMS officials stated that the T-MSIS project is in the midst of implementation with all states. Moreover, all states are working towards completion of the T-MSIS implementation in 2015, according to CMS. CMS went live with its federal T-MSIS platform in May 2015, and estimates that at least half the Medicaid population in the United States will be available through submitted T-MSIS files by the end of 2015.

However, officials from the four states included in our review told us that they are experiencing challenges with implementing T-MSIS requirements. Specifically, officials from three of the states explained that CMS continues to change data-field requirements for the data submissions.

MEDICAID PRESCRIPTION-DRUG CLAIMS DATA CONTAINED INDICATORS OF POTENTIAL FRAUD AND IMPROPER PAYMENTS IN FOUR SELECTED STATES

Our analysis of fiscal year 2011 Medicaid prescription claims data from four selected states identified several indicators of potential fraud.[29] Specifically, we found indicators of potential fraud among beneficiaries, prescribers, and pharmacies (1) with questionable patterns related to received, prescribed, and dispensed drugs; (2) who received drugs for certain conditions for which the beneficiaries had no other indicators in their fiscal year 2011 Medicaid outpatient claims; and (3) with concerns identified using data matching—such as prescribers who appeared to be deceased by the prescribed date. Because of the age of the data, we did not independently investigate individual transactions to confirm whether a particular beneficiary, prescriber, or pharmacy actually engaged in fraud, waste, or abuse.[30]

Questionable Patterns Related to Drugs Received in Four Selected States Indicate Potential Fraud

Potentially Excessive Prescription Claims

Beneficiaries who receive large numbers of drugs, especially of the same drug, can indicate possible overutilization and, in more-egregious cases, drug diversion.[31] Additionally, beneficiaries obtaining services from many different prescribers can raise questions. In our analysis of potentially excessive prescription claims, we found the following:

- **Beneficiaries with high quantities of the same drug.** About 700 of the 5.4 million beneficiaries we reviewed received more than a 1-year supply (a 480-day supply) of the same drug in 2011 at a cost to Medicaid of at least $1.6 million.[32] About 50 of these beneficiaries received more than 2 years' worth (a 730-day supply) of the same drug. One beneficiary appeared to receive more than 3-1/2 years' worth of the same respiratory medication at a cost to Medicaid of at least $10,000. Another beneficiary received more than 1 year's worth of seven different drugs at a cost to Medicaid of at least $30,000.
- **Beneficiaries visiting five or more prescribers.** Doctor shopping is a beneficiary fraud scheme in which Medicaid beneficiaries visit

multiple prescribers to obtain more prescriptions for the same or similar drugs than a single physician would prescribe.[33] Specifically, when a beneficiary obtains drugs from many prescribers or pharmacies, it could mean the beneficiary is seeking drugs to divert for profit or that the beneficiary's identification number was stolen. Another concern is that the beneficiary is getting excessive doses or supplies. According to CMS data, more than 16,000 beneficiaries out of the 5.4 million we reviewed visited five or more prescribers to receive prescriptions for antipsychotics or respiratory medications valued at about $33 million.[34] For example, a single beneficiary visited 15 prescribers and 10 pharmacies to obtain various antipsychotics at a cost to Medicaid of about $23,000 in 1 year. Another beneficiary received prescriptions for respiratory medications at 11 pharmacies written by 21 prescribers at a cost to Medicaid of at least $4,800 in 1 year. Table 1 shows the number of potential doctor shoppers and the costs associated with the purchased drugs for these therapeutic classes, by prescribers visited.[35]

Table 1. Estimated Number of Beneficiaries in Four Selected States Who Received Prescriptions for the Same Drug Class from Five or More Prescribers during Fiscal Year 2011

Drug class		Received prescriptions from 5 to 6 providers	Received prescriptions from 7 to 10 providers	Received prescriptions from 11 or more providers	Total
Antipsychotic	Number of beneficiaries	4,800	850	30	5,720
	Cost (dollars in thousands)	$17,200	$3,400	$224	$20,865
Respiratory	Number of beneficiaries	9,100	1,560	90	10,730
	Cost (dollars in thousands)	$10,100	$2,300	$163	$12,620
Total	Number of beneficiaries	13,900	2,400	130	16,440
	Cost (dollars in thousands)	$27,400	$5,700	$387	$33,485

Source: GAO analysis of Arizona, Florida, Michigan, and New Jersey data. | GAO-15-390.
Note: Totals do not add up due to rounding.

Beneficiaries may have a justifiable reason for receiving prescriptions from multiple medical practitioners. For example, a beneficiary may legitimately receive prescriptions from different prescribers within the same practice. Also if a beneficiary moves multiple times over the course of the year, he or she may still require the same prescriptions, which will necessitate visits to additional prescribers. There may be other legitimate medical reasons for receiving prescriptions for the same drug from multiple prescribers, such as visiting multiple specialists.

Questionable Prescribing and Dispensing Patterns

Analysis of prescribing and dispensing patterns can also help identify indicators of potential fraud, waste, and abuse. Excessive patterns of prescribing or dispensing, relative to peers, can indicate potential fraud. For example, we examined and identified prescribers and pharmacies with an unusually high proportion of activity for brand-name drugs.[36] In addition, analysis of pharmacy adjustments on claims can indicate whether pharmacies are properly billing Medicaid. In our analysis of prescription claims for questionable prescribing and dispensing patterns, we found the following:

- **Prescribers and pharmacies associated with high numbers of brand-name drugs.** In our discussions with officials that had investigated or researched prescription-drug fraud, we found that brand-name drugs can be at greater risk of diversion due to their relatively high expense. In more egregious examples, an unusually high proportion of brand-name drugs could represent a kickback scheme benefitting the prescriber or indicate a substitution of generic drugs scheme where the pharmacy dispenses generics but bills for more-expensive brand-name drugs.[37] Our analysis identified 119 out of about 28,000 prescribers associated with at least 500 claims for which at least 75 percent of the prescriptions were written for brand-name drugs. Among the 8,800 pharmacies we reviewed with at least 500 claims, we found about 300 pharmacies for which over half of the prescriptions filled were for brand-name drugs. We also found 37 pharmacies with at least 500 claims that only dispensed brand-name drugs.[38]
- **Pharmacies without adjustments.** When a change to a prescription is made or when a beneficiary fails to pick up the prescribed drugs, the pharmacy must adjust the claim transaction. According to officials in New Jersey, instances of pharmacies with too many or too few

adjustments may be red flags for concern. We identified about 70 out of approximately 4,000 pharmacies that filed over 5,000 claims without a single adjustment. These pharmacies received at least $23 million from Medicaid during fiscal year 2011. In contrast, among pharmacies that filled over 5,000 claims, the median pharmacy adjusted about 2 percent of its claims and the mean pharmacy adjusted about 5 percent of its claims. As we stated previously, adjustments may reflect changes to claims for medications that are not picked up by beneficiaries. While there may be legitimate reasons for a pharmacy to have low percentages of adjustments to claims, such pharmacies may warrant follow-up review by state oversight officials. For example, Michigan officials stated that there are some long-term nursing care facilities that only bill for the medications consumed by patients at the end of the month. These facilities would not have adjustments in their claims because the bill at the end of the month reflects the accurate amount of medication used by the patient.

Beneficiaries in Four Selected States Receiving Drugs for Conditions Not Identified in Their Fiscal Year 2011 Medicaid Outpatient Claims Indicate Potential Improper Payments

We identified beneficiaries in our four selected states who received prescription drugs only used to treat HIV and medications primarily used to treat diabetes but who had no additional (beyond receiving the HIV or diabetes medications) indicators of HIV or diabetes in their outpatient Medicaid activity from fiscal year 2011.[39] The absence of such evidence does not prove that the beneficiary did not have HIV or diabetes or that there was inappropriate off-label use:[40] the claims files we used were for a limited period and did not reflect the beneficiary's entire medical history, and our search may not have included every possible diagnosis or service code related to HIV and diabetes.[41]

HIV Medications Prescribed to Beneficiaries without Indicators of HIV in Their Fiscal Year 2011 Medicaid Outpatient Claims

The HHS OIG reported in August 2014 that antiretroviral drugs that treat HIV are a target for fraud, waste, and abuse because they can be very expensive and can have psychoactive effects.[42] Our analysis showed that the majority (94 percent) of the approximately 13,000 beneficiaries who received prescriptions for one of five HIV drug treatments had an HIV-related diagnosis indicator documented in their fiscal year 2011 Medicaid outpatient claims. In contrast, more than 750 of the 13,000 beneficiaries received HIV medications despite having no apparent indicator of having HIV in their fiscal year 2011 Medicaid outpatient claims. These beneficiaries received the HIV medications Atripla, Combivir, Norvir, Reyataz, and Truvada, which according to Food and Drug Administration indications and usage labeling are used to treat HIV-positive patients.

Table 2. Estimated Costs Associated with Beneficiaries in Four Selected States in Fiscal Year 2011 Who Received Human Immunodeficiency Virus (HIV) Medications but Did Not Have Outpatient Claims in Fiscal Year 2011 Indicating HIV

HIV drug	Beneficiaries with 1 to 11 claims		Beneficiaries with 12 or more claims	
	Number of beneficiaries	Medicaid paid amount (dollars in thousands)	Number of beneficiaries	Medicaid paid amount (dollars in thousands)
Atripla	190	$728	30	$418
Combivir	80	114	20	85
Norvir	280	283	60	155
Reyataz	140	348	40	215
Truvada	310	853	60	523
Total	640	$2,326	140	$1,397

Source: GAO analysis of Arizona, Florida, Michigan, and New Jersey data. | GAO-15-390.

Note: Totals do not add up because beneficiaries may receive multiple medications. The claims files we used were for a limited period and did not reflect the beneficiary's entire medical history. Therefore, we cannot determine from data analysis alone which cases represent inappropriate prescriptions and which are permissible prescribing patterns.

Medicaid paid about $3.7 million in claims for HIV medications for beneficiaries with no other indications in their fiscal year 2011 outpatient claims of having HIV. For example, 60 beneficiaries each received Truvada at least 12 times despite not having a HIV diagnosis code or other indicator for HIV, costing Medicaid at least $523,000. About 30 beneficiaries with no HIV indicators each received the HIV medication Atripla at least 12 times at a cost to Medicaid of at least $418,000.

One such beneficiary had 52 claims for multiple different HIV medications at a cost to Medicaid of over $50,000. Our analysis found that about 20 pharmacies dispensed HIV medications to at least 10 different beneficiaries who had no HIV indicators according to their fiscal year 2011 Medicaid claims. Table 2 summarizes the costs associated with each drug under review received by beneficiaries who did not have a Medicaid HIV indicator in the fiscal year 2011 outpatient claims file, broken out by beneficiaries with 1 to 11 claims and beneficiaries with 12 or more claims.

We cannot determine from data analysis alone which cases represent inappropriate prescriptions and which permissible prescribing patterns are. Such determinations would require additional review of the facts and circumstances of each individual case by state oversight officials.

Diabetes Medications Prescribed to Beneficiaries without Indicators of Diabetes in Their Fiscal Year 2011 Medicaid Outpatient Claims

Our analysis showed that the majority (96 percent) of the approximately 57,000 beneficiaries who received prescriptions for one of four diabetes treatments had diabetes-related indicators elsewhere in their fiscal year 2011 Medicaid outpatient claims. However, we identified about 2,300 beneficiaries who received diabetes medications, including Actos, Humalog, Lantus, and Novolog, without other indicators for the disease in their Medicaid outpatient claims.

The costs for providing these medications amounted to at least $680,000. For example, about 100 beneficiaries each received 12 or more prescriptions for Actos at a total cost to Medicaid of at least $96,000. Another 72 beneficiaries each received 12 or more prescriptions for Lantus costing Medicaid at least $46,000. Table 3 summarizes the costs associated with each drug under review received by beneficiaries who did not have a diabetes-related indicator in the fiscal year 2011 outpatient claims file, broken out by beneficiaries with 1 to 11 claims and beneficiaries with 12 or more claims.

We cannot determine from data analysis alone which cases represent inappropriate prescriptions and which represent permissible prescribing patterns or anomalies within the data. Again, such determinations would require additional review of the facts and circumstances of each individual case by oversight officials.

Table 3. Estimated Costs Associated with Beneficiaries in Four Selected States in Fiscal Year 2011 Who Received Certain Diabetes Medications but Did Not Have Outpatient Claims in Fiscal Year 2011 Related to the Disease

Diabetes drug	Beneficiaries with 1 to 11 claims		Beneficiaries with 12 or more claims	
	Number of beneficiaries	Medicaid paid amount (dollars in thousands)	Number of beneficiaries	Medicaid paid amount (dollars in thousands)
Actos	600	$191	100	$96
Humalog	520	149	20	32
Lantus	1,210	161	70	46
Novolog	410	13	10	0
Total	2,160	$514	190	$174

Source: GAO analysis of Arizona, Florida, Michigan, and New Jersey data. | GAO-15-390.

Note: Totals do not add up because beneficiaries may receive multiple medications. The claims files we used were for a limited period and did not reflect the beneficiary's entire medical history. Therefore, we cannot determine from data analysis alone which cases represent inappropriate prescriptions and which are permissible prescribing patterns.

Indicators of Potential Improper Payments Identified Using Data Matching

Of the 5.4 million beneficiaries in the four states we examined, we found hundreds of cases from the fiscal year 2011 data that showed potential indicators of improper payments, which may include fraudulent activity (e.g., prescriptions written by apparently deceased prescribers), due to concerns about the beneficiary, prescriber, or pharmacy. Figure 1 summarizes the results of our matching data to external sources to identify indicators of potential improper payments or fraud. Additional investigation would be required to definitively determine whether improper payment or fraud occurred.

Indicators of potentially fraudulent or abusive activities relating to prescription drugs
GAO found indicators of potentially fraudulent or abusive activities related to prescription drugs, including prescriptions written by or for deceased, incarcerated, and excluded individuals, as well as patients receiving prescriptions from more than one state.

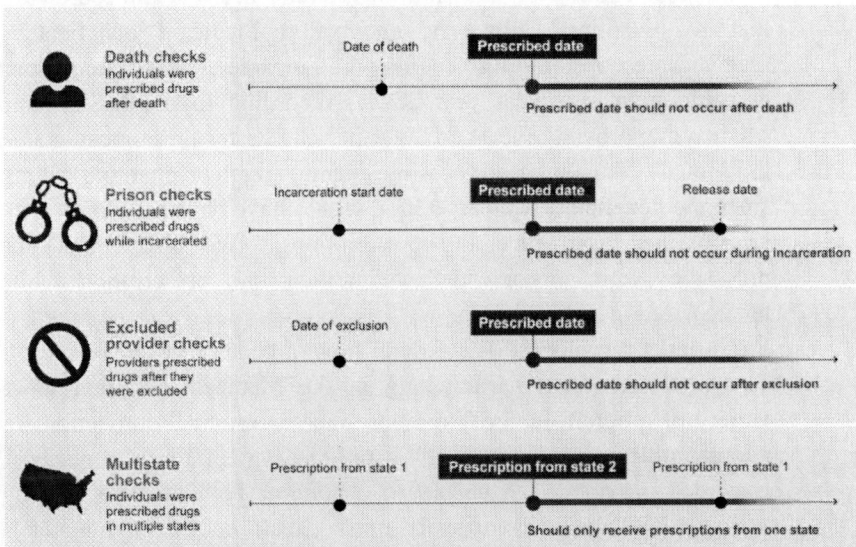

Source: GAO analysis of Centers for Medicare & Medicaid Services (CMS), General Services Administration (GSA), Department of Health and Human Services (HHS), Social Security Administration (SSA), and state data. | GAO-15-390.

Note: Data are from the Medicaid Statistical Information System (MSIS), Excluded Parties List System, List of Excluded Individuals and Entities, Social Security Administration (SSA) death data, and state prison records.

Figure 1. Potential Improper-Payment Indicators Related to Medicaid Claims for Prescription Medication for Four Selected States during Fiscal Year 2011.

- **Deceased prescribers.** The identities of 290 deceased prescribers in the four states we examined were used to prescribe drugs to individuals who received Medicaid benefits. The cost of the drugs totaled at least $77,000 for fiscal year 2011.[43]
- **Deceased beneficiaries.** The identities of about 170 deceased beneficiaries in the four states we examined were used to obtain prescriptions that were subsequently filled and paid for by Medicaid. The cost of the drugs totaled at least $32,000 for fiscal year 2011.[44]
- **Incarcerated beneficiaries and prescribers.** Federal law prohibits states from obtaining federal Medicaid matching funds for health-care services provided to inmates, with the exception of inmates who are patients in medical institutions. The intent of the federal prohibition is

to ensure that federal Medicaid funds are not used to finance care that is the responsibility of state and local authorities. For the four states that we examined, however, about 200 Medicaid beneficiaries received prescription-drug benefits while incarcerated in state prisons at some point in fiscal year 2011. According to the MSIS data, Medicaid approved at least $41,000 in benefits for these incarcerated individuals. This suggests possible identity theft or phantom billing since the beneficiary's incarceration would have physically prevented him or her from receiving prescriptions.[45] We also found one prescriber who appears to have written one prescription while incarcerated in a state prison.

- **Excluded prescribers.** The federal government can exclude health-care providers from participating in the Medicaid program for a variety of program-integrity reasons, such as criminal convictions or major problems related to health care (e.g., patient abuse or neglect). Excluded providers can be placed on one or both of the following lists, which Medicaid officials must check before paying for a prescription claim: the List of Excluded Individuals and Entities, managed by HHS, and the System for Award Management, managed by GSA.[46] The primary effect of these exclusions is that no payment will be provided for any items or services furnished, ordered, or prescribed by an excluded individual or entity. This includes Medicare, Medicaid, and all other federal plans and programs that provide health benefits funded directly or indirectly by the United States. We found about 200 excluded prescribers who wrote prescriptions that were then used to obtain prescription drugs that were paid for by Medicaid. The selected states approved and paid the claims at a cost of over $1 million.[47]

- **Beneficiaries concurrently receiving benefits in two or more states.** Beneficiaries are entitled to Medicaid prescription-drug benefits in the states in which they currently reside but are not eligible to receive Medicaid benefits in more than one state concurrently.[48] We identified about 618 beneficiaries that received prescription drugs from Medicaid in two or more of our selected states concurrently. The costs associated with these drugs were at least $186,000.

DRUG UTILIZATION REVIEWS HELP STATES DETECT AND PREVENT UNNECESSARY PRESCRIPTIONS, AND ADDITIONAL REPORTING WOULD HELP CMS DETERMINE WHETHER MORE GUIDANCE ON CONTROLS IS NEEDED

CMS monitors state Medicaid programs' efforts to prevent and detect instances of prescription-drug fraud in Medicaid, but we identified areas that may require additional guidance for oversight. Required by federal law, the Medicaid Drug Utilization Review (DUR) program is one process states use to promote patient safety and monitor prescription-drug activity for fraud, waste, and abuse.[49] In the first phase (prospective DUR) the states use tools such as point-of-sale edits, preferred-drug lists, and eligibility screening to promote patient safety and avoid abuse. The second phase (retrospective DUR) involves ongoing and periodic examination of claims data to identify patterns of fraud, abuse, gross overuse, or medically unnecessary care and implements corrective action when needed. For example, these measures can include postpayment reviews, lock-in programs, and pharmacy automatic refill restrictions.[50] An effective DUR can reduce states' exposure to potential fraud schemes, such as those described earlier in this report.[51] Federal statute and regulation require that states report on their DUR activities as well as cost savings generated from their DUR programs.[52]

CMS also collects information from states about DUR program operations, cost savings from DUR programs, and innovative DUR practices by means of the Medicaid Drug Utilization Review Annual Report Survey. CMS compiles this information into an annual summary report that is publicly available, and may be used to highlight innovative practices that state Medicaid programs have implemented.

According to the fiscal year 2013 Medicaid Drug Utilization Review State Comparison Annual Report (2013 CMS DUR Summary), DUR activities saved an average of about 18 percent on drug costs, adding up to about $3.9 billion in savings. CMS does not collect information about lock-in programs for noncontrolled substances or automatic refill prohibitions, despite the concerns detailed below.

Prospective DUR

Prospective DUR screens prescription-drug claims to identify possible safety and overuse indicators before the drugs are dispensed. Key prospective DUR controls include the following:

- **Point-of-sale edits.** Point-of-sale edits are alerts that occur at the pharmacy point of sale and promote patient safety and program integrity by sending alerts to pharmacies during the process of filling the prescription to determine whether certain criteria are met. Effective point-of-sale edits can address issues such as the potentially excessive and unnecessary prescriptions described earlier in this report. Alerts, such as drug–drug interactions or therapeutic duplication, appear when there is a drug interaction risk or when a patient is to be dispensed a drug that is in the same therapeutic class as another recently dispensed drug, respectively.[53] These alerts also work to promote patient safety as well as program integrity. A DUR can also include alerts such as a gender-specific alert that occurs when a drug is dispensed that is not recommended for use by the gender indicated on the recipient's eligibility file. Other alerts such as early-refill warnings are routine edits that may signal that the patient is not taking the drug according to the directions or may be misusing the medication. Early-refill alerts also help to prevent Medicaid from paying for excessive amounts of medication above and beyond what is necessary. According to the 2013 CMS DUR Summary, all states set early-refill thresholds as a way of preventing prescriptions from being refilled too soon, which is categorized as a point-of-sale edit.
- **Preferred-drug list.** DUR often include a preferred-drug list, which is designed to help keep health-care costs down by encouraging use of preferred, generic and over-the-counter drugs. The preferred-drug list drives a market shift to generic drugs when the generic drug pricing is less than the brand-name drug pricing (net of CMS and supplemental rebates), although prescribers can override the preferred-drug list using a prior-authorization request. Use of the preferred-drug list may limit or prevent wasteful spending.
- **Eligibility screening.** As described earlier in this report, states are to screen for the eligibility of beneficiaries, prescribers, pharmacies, and other entities to ensure that they have coverage under or participate in a health-insurance program. States are to use federal death sources

such as SSA's Death Master File as well as local sources such as the state's vital statistics office and prisoner files to check for the death and incarcerations of beneficiaries. Per CMS regulations, states are also required to use tools such as the List of Excluded Individuals and Entities, managed by HHS, and the System for Award Management, managed by GSA, to screen prescribing providers or pharmacies for federal exclusions and debarments.[54]

Retrospective DUR

Retrospective DUR involves ongoing and periodic examination of claims data to identify potentially problematic patterns. Key retrospective DUR fraud controls include postpayment reviews, lock-in programs, and automatic refill prohibitions.

- **Postpayment reviews.** Postpayment reviews involve reviewing claims and other documents after payment to ensure compliance with payment rules, and to determine whether the prescription was medically necessary. These reviews permit states to suspend payments and obtain and review medical records. Specific tactics states may choose to employ to find fraud in these payments include examining claims by amount paid, average costs, number of claims, adjustment rates, or percentage of claims for brand-name or Drug Enforcement Administration Schedule II drugs.[55] States can vary the period of review depending on available data and may monitor overall activity as well as activity within subsections of the population. For example, states can look for top beneficiary recipients of a certain drug or therapeutic class, prescribers who most frequently prescribe controlled substances, or pharmacies that dispense certain drugs at an average cost that is significantly higher than that of their peers. There are numerous ways the data can be analyzed and checks can be combined to strengthen detection of indicators of potential fraud. Effective strategies can then be repeated. While it is likely not possible to determine from data analysis alone whether any given prescription was appropriate, such analysis can detect anomalies that might warrant additional audit and investigation outside the DUR process. For example, as we discussed previously in this report, a pharmacy may dispense an unusually high proportion of brand-name medications. States can use pharmacy audits to ensure dispensary compliance with program rules and regulations while looking for fraud and abuse.

- **Lock-In Programs (also known as Restricted Recipient Programs).** As noted earlier in this report, we identified about 16,000 individuals whose visits to multiple prescribers for antipsychotics and respiratory medications raise questions.[56] Lock-in programs are one DUR tool that can address doctor shopping by locking beneficiaries who have abused the Medicaid program in to one prescriber, one pharmacy, or both for receiving prescriptions. Lock-in allows both prescribers and pharmacies to develop a more-complete picture of the beneficiary's drug-utilization history. Lock-in programs historically have applied to those beneficiaries in an FFS arrangement, although MCOs may employ similar measures to "lock-in" enrollees when such actions are warranted.

Lock-ins are typically triggered by abuse of controlled substances. Officials in Arizona and New Jersey stated that their lock-in program has historically focused on lock-in for controlled substances, although lock-ins for other drugs were permitted. Officials in Florida stated that their program does not use lock-in for noncontrolled substances and has trended towards using point-of-sale edits to restrict doctor-shopping activities related to controlled substances. Michigan officials stated that the state Medicaid program has two categories of lock-ins: beneficiaries may be locked in to a specific prescriber for controlled substances, or beneficiaries may be locked in to specific prescribers and pharmacies for all medications. Michigan officials indicated that they apply specific criteria to determine the lock-in category a beneficiary is assigned.

According to CMS officials, CMS does not have specific guidance for the state Medicaid programs on lock-ins. They said that states decide the requirement for placing a beneficiary in a lock-in program. Given that we found more than 16,000 beneficiaries who received prescriptions for relatively high-value medications from at least five prescribers in 1 fiscal year, there is a risk that Medicaid is wasting funds on prescriptions that are medically not necessary, and potentially fraudulently diverted. Although there is no federal requirement for states to implement a lock-in program, according to the 2013 CMS DUR Summary all but one of the states has a lock-in program for controlled substances. However, the report does not

contain information on lock-in programs for noncontrolled substances.
- **Pharmacy Automatic Refill.** Pharmacies may automatically refill prescriptions for certain medications without any customer action. Automatic refill services can be employed at both retail and mail-service pharmacies. In retail settings, medications that are not picked up by the patient within a finite period must be returned to stock. However, mail-service pharmacies are unable to return the medication to stock once the prescription is delivered. Concerns with pharmacy automatic refill include the potential for stockpiling, continued fill of discontinued medications, and an increase in the cost and waste of prescription medications. In 2013, CMS banned pharmacy automatic refills in the Medicare Part D program because these practices were potentially generating significant waste and unnecessary additional costs for the Medicare Part D program overall.

Unlike Medicare Part D, CMS currently does not have specific guidance on pharmacy automatic refills for the Medicaid program.[57]

CMS officials stated that policy on pharmacy automatic refills is a state-specific decision and states may have information in their billing instructions to pharmacies on their policy regarding automatic refills. In addition, CMS officials said that each state's Board of Pharmacy may have a policy on this subject and that these boards may audit pharmacies regarding their compliance with state regulations. Currently, Florida and Arizona are the states in our review that do not allow automatic refills. When asked why such prohibitions were in place, officials in Arizona noted that its Medicaid population was transient, and automatic refills could lead to prescriptions mailed to old addresses where the beneficiary no longer lived, at the state's expense. Officials in Florida cited concerns about beneficiaries stockpiling medications and not wanting to pay for prescriptions that were no longer needed.

Federal regulations define abuse as provider practices that are inconsistent with sound fiscal, business, or medical practices, and result in an unnecessary cost to the Medicaid program, or in reimbursement for services that are not medically necessary. Automatic refill programs may result in Medicaid beneficiaries obtaining medications far in excess of what was utilized or needed, resulting in wasted Medicaid resources. In fact, officials in New Jersey stated that automatic refills pose a problem for both fraud and waste of government funds, but at the time of our review did not have a policy preventing this practice.

According to the Standards for Internal Control in the Federal Government, internal controls should generally be designed to ensure that ongoing monitoring occurs in the course of normal operations, and that it is performed continually and ingrained in the agency's operations.[58] Our review of CMS monitoring activities found that CMS surveys states on a variety of different measures for fraud and waste prevention as well as cost-savings measures. Our discussions with officials in the selected states and CMS indicated that lock-in programs for noncontrolled substances and automatic refill prohibitions may warrant additional review. As discussed previously, state Medicaid programs varied in the type of medications that are included in lock-in programs. Additionally, we found more than 16,000 beneficiaries who received prescriptions for relatively high-value medications from at least five prescribers in 1 fiscal year, indicating that there is a risk that Medicaid is wasting funds on prescriptions that are medically not necessary, and potentially fraudulently diverted. The Medicare Part D program, as well as Florida and Arizona Medicaid programs, prohibit automatic refills, citing both patient safety and unnecessary costs as concerns for implementing these practices. However, CMS does not collect this information in the DUR survey or other collection methods. As a result, CMS does not know the number of state Medicaid programs that prohibit automatic refills or have lock-in programs for noncontrolled substances. Additional information would allow CMS to determine whether additional guidance for locking in recipients of noncontrolled substances and prohibiting automatic refills in Medicaid could prevent some of the problems we identified in our analysis and lead to cost savings.

CONCLUSION

Our review of fiscal year 2011 prescription-drug claims data from four states uncovered indicators of potential fraud, waste, and abuse throughout the Medicaid prescription-drug program in those states, including potential doctor shopping of noncontrolled substances. In addition, interviews with officials from these four states highlighted Medicaid practices that were prone to waste and abuse, such as pharmacy automatic refills. Ensuring that cost-effective controls are in place and working properly requires additional improvements from the MCOs, states, and CMS responsible for administering Medicaid. While CMS oversees the administration of state Medicaid programs, CMS does not currently identify whether states have implemented lock-in programs for noncontrolled substances or automatic refill prohibitions. Lock-in programs are an important tool that can be used to address doctor shopping by locking beneficiaries who have abused the Medicaid program in to one prescriber, one pharmacy, or both for receiving prescriptions. Automatic refill prohibitions may help limit waste and unnecessary program expenditures. Expanding monitoring efforts to examine these matters in greater depth would provide CMS with more-complete information to help determine whether there is a need to issue guidance to address these potential problems more consistently to help ensure greater program integrity and additional cost savings.

RECOMMENDATION FOR EXECUTIVE ACTION

To enhance monitoring of potentially wasteful or abusive practices in the Medicaid program, we recommend that the Acting Administrator of CMS require states to report to CMS whether their state has lock-in programs for abusers of noncontrolled substances and prohibitions on pharmacy automatic refills, and examine the results to determine whether additional guidance is appropriate.

AGENCY COMMENTS AND OUR EVALUATION

We provided a draft copy of this report to HHS, SSA, and state Medicaid program offices for Arizona, Florida, Michigan, and New Jersey. Written comments from HHS; SSA; the Arizona Health Care Cost Containment System (AHCCCS); the Florida Agency for Health Care Administration (AHCA); and the State of New Jersey, Department of Human Services, Division of Medical Assistance and Health Services (DMAHS) are summarized below. HHS concurred with our recommendation. The letter from SSA stated the agency had no comments on our report. AHCCCS disagreed with our methodology and provided detailed comments on our findings, as described below. AHCA did not comment on the report's findings but stated that the state Medicaid program already prohibits pharmacy automatic refills and will work with CMS to implement a lock-in program for noncontrolled substance abusers. DMAHS did not comment on the report's findings but outlined several steps the state has taken that could address the types of issues raised in our report, which are summarized below. In an e-mail received on May 28, 2015, officials from the Michigan Department of Community Health did not comment on the report's findings but provided technical comments, which we incorporated as appropriate. In addition, we provided excerpts of this draft report related to the reliability issues of Medicaid data to state Medicaid program offices for California, Illinois, Maryland, New York, Ohio, Pennsylvania, and Texas for technical comment. In an e-mail received on May 19, 2015, the Deputy Director, Division of Program Development and Management of the New York Department of Health, provided suggestions regarding CMS's implementation of T-MSIS, which was outside the scope of our review, so we did not incorporate these comments in our draft report. Officials from California, Illinois, Maryland, New York, Ohio, Pennsylvania, and Texas did not provide technical comments.

In its written comments, HHS concurred with our recommendation and stated that it will consider requiring states to report on lock-in programs for abusers of noncontrolled substances and pharmacy automatic refill policies. HHS also outlined the steps the agency has taken to improve data collection in Medicaid and address prescription-medication fraud since the fiscal year 2011 data used in our study. We incorporated these comments in our report as appropriate.

In its written comments, AHCCCS said that it takes exception to being included in a series of findings that offer no state-specific detail. As we noted in our meetings with all state agencies included in our study, we did not provide state-level detail for two primary reasons. First, because CMS was the audited agency for our work, conducting analysis at the state-level would be outside the scope of our work and would put the focus on a comparison between the states, rather than on CMS oversight. In addition, due to the age and limitations of the data, as noted in the report, we would not be referring specific cases for follow-up. Moreover, AHCCCS noted that the findings of our study represent less than one-tenth of Medicaid spending for the four states used in our study. As we stated previously in this report, all of the states in our study had MCO arrangements in place during our study period. As a result, the Medicaid paid amounts associated with managed care may not be reflected in the state claims that were submitted to CMS for medical services, and hence our estimate is likely understated.

AHCCCS also commented on specific sections of our analysis. First, AHCCCS stated that our report did not identify state practices that are able to leverage more-accurate data sources on a real-time basis. As mentioned above, the focus of our work was CMS oversight of the Medicaid program rather than an in-depth discussion of current, specific practices employed by the states. Second, AHCCCS incorrectly stated that we used the federal incarceration file in our analysis. As we note in appendix I, we used each state's department of corrections prisoner databases for individuals incarcerated for any period during fiscal year 2011. Specifically, for our work, we used the same Arizona Department of Corrections file to perform matches that AHCCCS outlined in its response letter. Third, AHCCCS provided an overview of the additional checks the state performs to identify incarcerated beneficiaries, as well as deceased providers and beneficiaries. This overview does not refute the findings in our report, and we did not incorporate these details in the report.

Regarding our analysis of prescription-drug medication claims data, AHCCCS stated that our report should have used more than a single year of claims data to identify diagnosis information. We acknowledge this limitation, and updated our report with the appropriate caveats. Specifically, we state that we identified beneficiaries who did not have indicators of HIV or diabetes in their outpatient Medicaid activity from fiscal 2011, and that the absence of such evidence does not prove that the beneficiary does not have HIV or diabetes or that there was inappropriate off-label use. Further we stated that the results of this analysis may also be caused by off-label use, record-keeping, or data-coding issues. In addition, we noted that timing differences in the prior-authorization process could explain some of these observations. We also note that we cannot determine from data analysis alone which cases represent inappropriate prescriptions and which are permissible prescribing patterns.

Regarding our analysis of brand-name medications, AHCCCS stated that our findings represent 0.425 percent of prescribing clinicians. In the draft report provided to AHCCCS, we provided the number of individuals we found and the total study population to provide the appropriate context. AHCCCS also noted that our report did not take into consideration that states may continue to require brand-name coverage because it may be more costly to the state to purchase the generic product. As a result, we incorporated discussion of this limitation in our report. Similarly, AHCCCS stated that our report does not differentiate between retail pharmacies and specialty pharmacies, and that some specific specialty pharmacies are expected to have a high percentage of branded medications. We noted that we did not control for medications where there was not a generic version available. However, to address the specific concern of AHCCCS, we incorporated this caveat into our report. Again, as noted several times in our report, the results of our analysis are indicators of potential fraudulent or improper payments.

AHCCCS further stated that Arizona protocols already apply the recommendations in our report. In our report, we note that Arizona has a lock-in program that can incorporate noncontrolled medications and prohibits automatic refills in the Medicaid program. As noted in our report, the recommendation is addressed to CMS, and not the states used in our study. Specifically, we recommended that CMS collect information on what other states' practices are related to lock-ins of noncontrolled medications and prohibitions of automatic refills, and examine the results to determine whether additional guidance is appropriate.

Finally, AHCCCS stated that our report reaches sweeping conclusions without validating findings based on state-specific data. Again, as mentioned earlier, the focus of our report is CMS oversight of the Medicaid program. Our report provides the appropriate context for our findings, including limitations of our analysis to ensure that the results of our analysis were not taken in an inappropriate context.

In response to our draft report, the Florida Agency for Health Care Administration (AHCA) stated that the Florida Medicaid program currently does not allow pharmacy automatic refills. Further AHCA stated that it will work with CMS's guidance and recommendations for the implementation of a lock-in program for abusers of noncontrolled substances.

In its response to our draft report, the New Jersey Department of Human Services, Division of Medical Assistance and Health Services (DMAHS), stated that automatic prescription refills are a major concern for the State of New Jersey. According to DMAHS, although characterized by retail pharmacies as a "patient-friendly" service designed to improve the quality of prescription services, automatic prescription refills pose several concerns, such as the potential for stockpiling medications; continued filling of discontinued medications; unrecognized changes in drug therapies; and increases in fraud, waste, and abuse of prescription drugs. DMAHS stated that it looked forward to better understanding the audit practices used by CMS and certain states to audit this practice.

In addition, DMAHS outlined steps the New Jersey Medicaid program has taken to strengthen prescription-drug internal controls, including requiring MCO programs to implement a pharmacy lock-in program. DMAHS also provided comments to address additional actions the state has taken that would address the findings we outlined in our report, including a quality-management and utilization-review program that focuses on medical encounters and a quarterly doctor-shopper report that identifies recipients who may be engaged in fraudulent activities. While we did not make any specific recommendations to the states, we believe that such actions should enhance their oversight of prescription-drug controls.

Additionally, DMAHS provided comments on timely submission of MSIS data and stated that timely submission of MSIS data is related to the time required for CMS to validate New Jersey claims file submissions. We incorporated its comments in our report, as appropriate.

Seto J. Bagdoyan
Director, Audit Services
Forensic Audits and Investigative Service

APPENDIX I: OBJECTIVES, SCOPE, AND METHODOLOGY

In this report, we (1) evaluated the reliability of Medicaid data from the Centers for Medicare & Medicaid (CMS) and selected states for the purpose of identifying indicators of potential fraud or abuse; (2) identified and analyzed indicators, if any, of potentially fraudulent or abusive activities related to prescription drugs in Medicaid; and (3) examined the extent to which federal and selected state oversight policies, controls, and processes are designed to prevent and detect indicators of prescription-drug fraud in Medicaid.

To evaluate the reliability of Medicaid data from CMS for our selected states that could be used to identify indicators of potential fraud or abuse, we took several steps. We vetted 11 states for possible inclusion in our study.[1] We selected states based on high Medicaid beneficiary enrollment, geographic diversity, and availability of data. In the selection process, we also considered whether drugs were paid under fee-forservice (FFS) or managed care, by including states that included these program types in our review. We performed electronic testing to determine the validity of specific data elements in the federal and selected state databases that we used to perform our work. We also reviewed related documentation, including data layouts and agency reports. Specifically, we used a January 2013 Mathematica Policy Research report that details Medicaid Statistical Information System (MSIS) state data characteristics and anomalies to further vet states selected for our audit work.[2] We also used published GAO and Department of Health and Human Services (HHS) Office of the Inspector General (OIG) reports that detailed the limitations of the MSIS data we used for our study.[3] Additionally, we interviewed officials responsible for their respective databases to discuss data-reliability considerations, and reviewed prior work related to the quality of the MSIS data used for our study.[4] On the basis of our discussions with agency officials and our own testing, we concluded that the data elements from the four states— Arizona, Florida, Michigan and New Jersey—used for this report were sufficiently reliable for the purpose of identifying indicators of potential fraud or abuse. However, in assessing the reliability of the data, we observed reportable shortcomings such as issues with timeliness, completeness, and accuracy in the data that may affect Medicaid administrators' ability to effectively oversee their program. We discuss these shortcomings in greater detail earlier in this report.

To identify indicators of potentially fraudulent or abusive activities related to prescription drugs in Medicaid, we obtained and analyzed Medicaid claims paid in fiscal year 2011, the most-recent period from which we could draw reliable data, for four states: Arizona, Florida, Michigan and New Jersey. These states accounted for about 13 percent of the federal share of fiscal year 2011 Medicaid expenditures. These states were selected primarily because they had consistently comparable and reliable data and were among the states with the highest Medicaid expenditures. The results of our analysis of these states are not generalizable to other states.

We obtained CMS MSIS beneficiary, provider, prescription-drug, and other services claims data, as well as state Medicaid Management Information Systems (MMIS) crosswalk data (with personal identifiers) to perform our work. The crosswalk data we used contained specific identifying information on prescribers, pharmacies, and beneficiaries that were not collected in the MSIS data, such as name and address. Additionally, managed-care organizations (MCO) receive a monthly capitated payment.[5] As a result, the Medicaid paid amounts associated with managed care may not be reflected in the state claims that were submitted to CMS for medical services, and hence our estimate is likely understated. All of the states included in our review— Arizona, Florida, Michigan, and New Jersey—had MCO arrangements in place.

We reviewed literature related to health-care fraud, including reports discussing fraud, waste, and abuse related to prescription drugs. We interviewed federal, state, and private-sector auditors, program administrators, and other relevant officials who had published work that investigated or researched prescription-drug fraud. On the basis of this research, we identified areas at greater risk of fraud and abuse such as drugs at high risk for diversion and types of prescribing patterns that warranted additional review. We used this information to develop our analytic approach to identify indicators of potential fraud and abuse related to prescription drugs in Medicaid. To identify potential overuse, we reviewed beneficiaries who received more than a 480-day supply of the same medication in a single year based on the national drug code. To identify potential doctor-shopping activities, we examined beneficiaries who received prescriptions for drugs within one of two therapeutic classes of drugs from five or more prescribers. We focused on beneficiaries who received prescriptions for antipsychotics or respiratory medications from five or more different prescribers over the course of 1 year. We selected medications in these therapeutic classes because they had a large number of individuals who received drugs from five or more prescribers relative to other classes of noncontrolled substances we considered, have a known diversion risk, and are relatively expensive.[6] We selected the five-or-more prescribers threshold based on our review of drug-diversion literature and prior GAO work. Since we did not focus on all noncontrolled substances, our analysis understates the number of instances and dollar amounts related to potential doctor-shopping activities. We also looked for prescribers and pharmacies with a high proportion of prescribing or dispensing activities for brand-name drugs (versus generics) compared to the average activity of other prescribers and pharmacies[7] and pharmacies without any adjusted or voided claims.[8]

To identify potentially unnecessary prescription-drug activities, we reviewed claims paid on behalf of beneficiaries who received human immunodeficiency virus (HIV) and diabetes medications despite having no HIV or diabetes-related indicators related to such ailments in their fiscal year 2011 Medicaid outpatient claims listed in the MSIS "other services" file. The absence of such evidence does not prove that the beneficiary did not have HIV or diabetes or that there was inappropriate off-label use: the claims files we used were for a limited period and did not reflect the beneficiary's entire history, and our search may not have included every possible diagnosis or service code related to HIV and diabetes. We selected the HIV medications Atripla, Combivir, Norvir, Reyataz, and Truvada based on their specific use as a treatment for HIV as well as a preliminary examination of the MSIS data. We selected the diabetes medications Actos, Humalog, Lantus, and Novolog based on their primary use as a treatment for diabetes as well as a similar review of the MSIS data. We selected these drugs and drug classes because they were received by a relatively large number of beneficiaries and had a high expense to Medicaid. In addition, when we examined the Food and Drug

Administration indications and usage labeling for each drug, we found that each drug was only approved for treatment of HIV or diabetes.[9] For each beneficiary who received one of these drugs, we reviewed the MSIS "other services" file to determine whether the beneficiary (1) had an International Classification of Diseases diagnosis code related to HIV or diabetes, (2) had a Healthcare Common Procedure Coding System service code related to HIV or diabetes, or (3) had claims associated with the prescribing physician.[10] We removed beneficiaries from our analysis if they exhibited one of these characteristics and reported on the remaining population. We restricted our review to only include beneficiaries who received at least one prescription written during fiscal year 2011.

We also matched the Medicaid data to other external sources to identify potential fraud and improper payments. We compared the beneficiary and prescriber identity information shown in the Medicaid claims data to the Social Security Administration's (SSA) complete file of death information from October 2012 to determine whether any individuals were reportedly deceased before or when they purportedly prescribed, dispensed, or received prescription drugs covered by Medicaid. To identify prescription-drug claims that might have been improperly processed and paid by the Medicaid program because either the prescribers or beneficiaries were incarcerated, we matched our selected states' MMIS data to the states' departments of corrections prisoner databases. Prisoner data included individuals incarcerated for any period during fiscal year 2011. For Arizona, Florida, and New Jersey, we identified provider and beneficiary records for which the Medicaid Social Security number (SSN) and names matched that of a person who was incarcerated in fiscal year 2011 in any of the four states. Michigan did not provide SSNs in its incarceration data. For Michigan, we identified provider and beneficiary records for which the Medicaid name and birth day exactly matched that of a person who was incarcerated in fiscal year 2011 in any of the four states. We then identified Medicaid claims associated with the identified individuals by matching to the MSIS data. We compared the beginning service date of the claims to the individual's admittance and release date to identify all claims that occurred while the associated beneficiary or provider identity was incarcerated. Additionally, we reviewed these claims' type of service to determine that none qualified for federal matching funds.

It is not possible to determine from data matching alone whether these matches definitively identify recipients who were deceased or incarcerated without reviewing the facts and circumstances of each case. For example, it is possible that individuals can be erroneously listed in the full Death Master

File. Similarly, a provider or beneficiary may have an SSN, name, and date of birth similar to an individual in state prison records. Alternatively, our matches may also understate the number of deceased or incarcerated individuals receiving assistance because matching would not detect applicants whose identifying information in the Medicaid data differed slightly from their identifying information in other databases.

To identify Medicaid beneficiaries who received benefits in two or more states concurrently, we identified all beneficiary SSNs that appeared in two or more states' MMIS data in fiscal year 2011. We then found all claims associated with the beneficiary identities. We conducted further analysis to determine the states in which each beneficiary identity appeared and the service ranges—first and last prescribed date—for those states. We defined a concurrent claim as a claim that occurred within the service range of a second state for the same beneficiary identity. For each claim, we compared its prescription date to the service ranges for the beneficiary identity to determine whether it was a concurrent claim. It is not possible to definitely say through data matching alone that a beneficiary was improperly receiving Medicaid benefits in two or more states concurrently without looking into further information for each claim and beneficiary. For example, a beneficiary could have been a resident in one state and received services, then changed residency to a second state and received benefits for a brief period, before finally relocating again back to the original state and receiving additional services. In this case, the claims could have been identified as a concurrent claim even if the beneficiary did not receive any services from the original state during his or her relocation period in the second state.

To identify claims that might have been improperly processed and paid by the Medicaid program because the federal government had excluded these providers from providing services to Medicaid beneficiaries, we compared the Medicaid claims to the exclusion and debarment files from the Department of Health and Human Services' (HHS) Office of Inspector General (OIG) and the General Services Administration (GSA). Specifically, we used the HHS List of Excluded Individuals and Entities file from September 2012 and the GSA Excluded Parties List System database extract from October 2011 to perform our match. We matched MMIS and MSIS Medicaid data using SSN and individual name with both the List of Excluded Individuals and Entities and the Excluded Parties List System data extracts. We then identified unique individuals who had Medicaid claims processed where the date of exclusion occurred before the prescribed date in the Medicaid claims file.

To determine the extent to which federal and state oversight policies, controls, and processes are designed to prevent and detect instances of prescription-drug fraud in Medicaid, we reviewed CMS and state Medicaid policies pertinent to program integrity over pharmaceuticals, met with CMS officials, and visited state Medicaid offices that perform oversight functions for the four states we selected. We used federal standards for internal control,[11] GAO's Fraud Prevention Framework,[12] and Medicaid statutes and regulations addressing the administration of pharmacy benefits to evaluate these functions.

To determine the reliability of the data used in our analysis, we performed electronic testing to determine the validity of specific data elements in the federal and selected state databases that we used to perform our work. We also interviewed officials responsible for their respective databases, and reviewed documentation related to the databases and literature related to the quality of the data. On the basis of our discussions with agency officials and our own testing, we concluded that the data elements used for this report were sufficiently reliable for our purposes.

We identified criteria for Medicaid fraud controls by examining federal and state policies, laws, and guidance, including policy memos and manuals. We interviewed officials from CMS and the state governments of Arizona, Florida, Michigan, and New Jersey involved in Medicaid program administration, auditing, and Medicaid fraud response.

We conducted this performance audit from March 2014 to July 2015 in accordance with generally accepted government auditing standards. Those standards require that we plan and perform the audit to obtain sufficient, appropriate evidence to provide a reasonable basis for our audit findings and conclusions based on our audit objectives. We believe that the evidence obtained provides a reasonable basis for our findings and conclusions based on our audit objectives.

End Notes

[1] GAO has designated Medicaid as a high-risk program since 2003.

[2] An improper payment is defined by statute as any payment that should not have been made or that was made in an incorrect amount (including overpayments and underpayments) under statutory, contractual, administrative, or other legally applicable requirements.

[3] Fraud involves an intentional act or representation to deceive with the knowledge that the action or representation could result in gain. Waste includes inaccurate payments for services, such as unintentional duplicate payments. Abuse represents actions inconsistent with acceptable business or medical practices.

[4] GAO, *Medicaid: Fraud and Abuse Related to Controlled Substances Identified in Selected States*, GAO-09-957 (Washington, D.C.: Sept. 9, 2009).

[5] GAO, *Medicare Part D: Instances of Questionable Access to Prescription Drugs*, GAO-11-699 (Washington, D.C.: Sept. 6, 2011).

[6] The states vetted were: Arizona, California, Florida, Illinois, Maryland, Michigan, New Jersey, New York, Ohio, Pennsylvania, and Texas.

[7] Mathematica Policy Research, Inc., *MSIS State Data Characteristics/Anomalies Report* (Jan. 7, 2013).

[8] Department of Health and Human Services, Office of Inspector General, *Early Assessment of Review of Medicaid Integrity Contractors*, OEI-05-10-00200 (Washington, D.C.: February 2012). GAO, *National Medicaid Audit Program: CMS Should Improve Reporting and Focus on Audit Collaboration with States*, GAO-12-627 (Washington, D.C.: June 14, 2012); and *Medicaid: Data Sets Provide Inconsistent Picture of Expenditures*, GAO-13-47 (Washington, D.C.: Nov. 29, 2012).

[9] Mathematica Policy Research serves as CMS's contractor and performs reviews to ensure and report on the quality of MSIS data. The organization publishes information on unreconciled data in its anomalies report.

[10] MMIS crosswalk data contained information such as provider and beneficiary name and address. The quality of this information was not used to vet states for inclusion in this work.

[11] Drugs and other substances that are considered controlled substances under the Controlled Substances Act are divided into five schedules. An updated and complete list of the schedules is published annually in 21 C.F.R. §§ 1308.11 – 1308.15. Substances are placed in their respective schedules based on whether they have a currently accepted medical use in treatment in the United States, their relative abuse potential, and likelihood of causing dependence when abused. Drugs that are not considered controlled substances are known as noncontrolled substances.

[12] Our analysis did not control for medications where there was not a generic version available.

[13] When a change to a prescription is made or when a beneficiary fails to pick up the prescribed drugs, the pharmacy must adjust the claim transaction. According to officials in New Jersey, instances of pharmacies with too many or too few adjustments may be red flags for concern.

[14] This analysis was based on diagnosis codes for HIV or diabetes. We did not account for prescribing of these medications for other ailments.

[15] GAO, *Standards for Internal Control in the Federal Government*, GAO/AIMD-00-21.3.1 (Washington, D.C.: November 1999).

[16] GAO, *Individual Disaster Assistance Programs: Framework for Fraud Prevention, Detection, and Prosecution*, GAO-06-954T (Washington, D.C.: July 12, 2006).

[17] GAO-13-47. Changes to MSIS, including requirements for reporting time frames, began implementation in July 2014. The updated system is known as the Transformed Medicaid Statistical information System (T-MSIS).

[18] The False Claims Act prohibits certain actions, including the knowing presentation of a false claim for payment by the federal government. 31 U.S.C. § 3729(a)(1)(A).

[19] See for example: GAO, *Medicaid Program Integrity: Increased Oversight Needed to Ensure Integrity of Growing Managed Care Expenditures*, GAO-14-341 (Washington, D.C.: May 19, 2014); *Medicaid Program Integrity: CMS Pursues Many Practices to Address Prescription Drug Fraud, Waste, and Abuse*, GAO-15-66 (Washington, D.C.: Oct. 24, 2014); and Department of Health and Human Services, Office of Inspector General, *Part D Beneficiaries with Questionable Utilization Patterns for HIV Drugs*, OEI-02-11-00170 (Washington, D.C.: August 2014).

[20] GAO-15-66.

[21] The results of our data-reliability work are not generalizable to other states or time frames other than fiscal year 2011.

[22] State Medicaid officials from Illinois, New York, and Texas reported that their programs were shifting away from FFS to an MCO system. We excluded data from these three states because the most-recent data available (fiscal year 2011) would not reflect this transition and not because of data availability or quality concerns. We did not independently analyze data from California, Maryland, Ohio, or Pennsylvania to corroborate state officials' statements or findings in the January 2013 Mathematica Policy Research report.

[23] In response to a draft of this report, New Jersey Medicaid program officials stated that for New Jersey the concern regarding the timely submission of MSIS data is related solely to the time required for CMS to validate New Jersey claims file submissions. According to the New Jersey officials, CMS was validating the state's quarterly claims file submissions for calendar years 2012 and 2013 in calendar year 2014.

[24] At the time of our data request, the most-recent validated CMS claims data available for Michigan were from the second quarter of fiscal year 2013. However, for consistency in our analysis, we used fiscal year 2011 data for all states. The oldest claims in our data were paid in October 2010, more than 3 years before we received the last file in February 2014.

[25] GAO-13-47.

[26] GAO, *National Medicaid Audit Program: CMS Should Improve Reporting and Focus on Audit Collaboration with States*, GAO-12-627 (Washington, D.C.: June 14, 2012).

[27] Department of Health and Human Service, Office of Inspector General, *Early Outcomes Show Limited Progress for the Transformed Medicaid Statistical Information System*, OEI05-12-00610 (Washington, D.C.: September 2013).

[28] The HHS OIG 2015 Compendium of Unimplemented Recommendations did not provide a timeline for implementing this recommendation, but noted that CMS work in this area was ongoing from March 2014.

[29] We reviewed prescription-drug activity for about 5.4 million beneficiaries, 251,000 prescribers, and 26,000 pharmacies that received, prescribed, or dispensed prescriptions drugs paid for by Medicaid during fiscal year 2011. These counts are based solely on fields in the MSIS data so it is possible that a beneficiary, prescriber, or pharmacy with multiple records in the MSIS data may have been counted multiple times.

[30] The categories for our analysis are not mutually exclusive. Individuals may be included in more than one analysis detailed in the report.

[31] Drug diversion is the redirection of prescription drugs for illegitimate purposes. Data errors and legitimate need due to severe illness may also explain why certain beneficiaries received large quantities of drugs during our analysis.

[32] We calculated the days of supply using 365 days or 1 year's worth of Medicaid data based on the dispense date. While it is possible that the beneficiary had a legitimate medical reason for obtaining a high volume of drugs, we considered it to be potentially fraudulent or improper if the total was more than 480 days for the same drug. We used 480 days instead of 365 to allow for one 90 day prescription for use in the next fiscal year and because it was divisible by 30. This is also the threshold HHS OIG officials used in their work on HIV medications in Medicare Part D (see HHS OIG, OEI-02-11-00170).

[33] The excess drugs are then consumed by the beneficiary, often for recreational purposes, or are diverted to another party for financial gain. The Medicaid program incurs excessive costs for both the prescription drugs purchased during the doctor-shopping scheme as well as the associated office visits. Estimates suggest costs associated with the office and emergency

room visits used to illicitly obtain drugs by means of doctor shopping can cost 14 times more than the drugs themselves. In this regard, our prior work has shown that Medicaid is vulnerable to doctor shopping for controlled substances. See GAO-09-957.

[34] For this analysis, we focused on beneficiaries who received prescriptions for antipsychotics or respiratory medications from five or more different prescribers over the course of 1 year. We selected medications in these therapeutic classes because they had a large number of individuals who received drugs from five or more prescribers relative to other classes of noncontrolled substances we considered, had the strongest doctor-shopping indicators (among noncontrolled substances), have a known diversion risk, and are relatively expensive.

[35] We cannot determine from data analysis alone which cases represent actual doctor shoppers and which cases represent instances in which the beneficiary had a legitimate reason for visiting multiple prescribing physicians. However, certain cases have stronger fraud indicators than others, such as those cases in which more than one pharmacy is involved.

[36] Other possible patterns such as number of drugs prescribed per beneficiary or number of pharmacies filling their prescriptions can provide indications of prescribers that are more susceptible to fraud, waste, and abuse. In addition, pharmacies being billed extremely high numbers of drugs per beneficiary or per prescriber, extremely high cost per beneficiary or claim, or extremely high numbers of refills and adjustments relative to other pharmacies can also indicate potential fraud.

[37] Michigan Medicaid officials noted that Michigan state law prohibits Medicaid from requiring prescription-medication preauthorizations for brand-name medications for specific protected conditions, including HIV and transplant recipients. Arizona Medicaid officials stated that some states continue to require specific brand name medication coverage because it is more costly to the state to purchase the generic product.

[38] We identified about 27,800 prescribers and 8,800 pharmacies with at least 500 claims. For each prescriber with at least 500 claims, we measured the proportion of all prescriptions written that were brand-name drugs. The average proportion was 16.5 percent (median = 19.9 percent). For each pharmacy with at least 500 claims, we measured the proportion of all prescription dispensed that were brand-name drugs. The average proportion was 19.3 percent (median = 21.7 percent). Our analysis did not control for medications where there was not a generic version available. Additionally, Arizona Medicaid officials stated that some specific specialty pharmacies may be expected to have a high percentage of branded medications.

[39] We used the MSIS "other services" file to examine each beneficiary's Medicaid activity. We excluded beneficiaries who did not have any activity whatsoever in the MSIS other services file from this analysis. The MSIS other services file covers all Medicaid or Children's Health Insurance Program claims that are not included in the MSIS inpatient, long-term, or prescription-drug claims files. This includes payments for provider claims for all noninstitutional Medicaid services.

[40] Off-label use refers to the prescription of a medication for uses other than what the Food and Drug Administration has approved. Our review did not include all drugs that may be used to treat HIV or diabetes. See appendix I for additional details about our drug selection criteria.

[41] The results of this analysis may also be caused by off-label use, record-keeping, or data-coding issues. In addition, one state suggested that timing differences in its prior-authorization process could explain some of these observations.

[42] HHS OIG, OEI-02-11-00170.

[43] Michigan Medicaid officials stated that there are instances in which a dead prescriber may appear to be billing after the day of death. In their program, they stated that this is usually because another member of the physician's practice writes the prescription and the pharmacy does not update the physician information. Michigan officials have identified this clerical data error in their own review of deceased prescribers.

[44] These results only include claims where the prescribed date occurred after death.

[45] Identity theft is stealing identifying information from providers and patients and using it for nefarious purposes. Phantom billing is billing for prescription drugs (or other services) that were not provided to the beneficiary.

[46] 42 C.F.R. § 455.436(c)(2) requires states to check the List of Excluded Individuals and Entities and the Excluded Parties List System. However, GSA discontinued the Excluded Parties List System in 2012 and moved its content to the System for Award Management. In August 2012, CMS officials instructed states to use the System for Award Management instead of the Excluded Parties List System to fulfill their regulatory responsibilities.

[47] We also looked for pharmacies in the four states that had been excluded from federal healthcare programs including Medicaid, but did not find any that billed Medicaid for prescription drugs dispensed during fiscal year 2011.

[48] Our analysis may have included Medicaid beneficiaries who moved back and forth between two of the selected states who appropriately terminated their Medicaid benefits after each move. For example, officials in Florida suggested individuals who move in and out of the area may have accounted for a portion of this analysis.

[49] 42 U.S.C. § 1396r-8(g).

[50] Lock-in programs are one DUR tool that can address doctor shopping by locking beneficiaries who have abused the Medicaid program in to one prescriber, one pharmacy, or both for receiving prescriptions.

[51] For the purposes of this section, we examined CMS's oversight role of the entire Medicaid program (as opposed to just in the selected states). Observations presented in this section are derived from a review of key documents such as the 2013 Medicaid Drug Utilization Review State Comparison Annual Report, state DUR plans, and interviews with Medicaid officials from Arizona, Florida, Michigan, and New Jersey. Due to the scope of our review, we focused on DUR measures related to the prevention and detection of fraud, waste, and abuse.

[52] 42 U.S.C. § 1396r-8(g)(3)(D) and 42 C.F.R. § 456.712.

[53] A therapeutic duplication DUR alert identifies instances of prescribing multiple medications for the same medical symptom or indication without a clear distinction of when one agent should be administered over another. The drug-disease contraindication DUR alert is activated when a drug is prescribed for an individual who has a disease for which the drug may be harmful.

[54] 42 C.F.R. § 455.436(c)(2).

[55] States have other requirements they must meet, such as timely payment that would be examined in a postpayment review. Drugs, substances, and certain chemicals used to make drugs are classified into five distinct categories or schedules depending upon the drug's acceptable medical use and the drug's abuse or dependency potential. The abuse rate is a determinate factor in the scheduling of the drug. Schedule II drugs, substances, or chemicals are defined as drugs that have a high potential for abuse, a currently accepted medical use in treatment in the United States or a currently accepted medical use with severe restrictions, and abuse may lead to severe psychological or physical dependence. These drugs are also considered dangerous. Some examples of Schedule II drugs are: combination products with

less than 15 milligrams of hydrocodone per dosage unit (Vicodin), cocaine, methamphetamine, methadone, hydromorphone (Dilaudid), meperidine (Demerol), oxycodone (OxyContin), fentanyl, Dexedrine, Adderall, and Ritalin.

[56] As noted earlier, we recognize that in some cases legitimate reasons exist to visit multiple prescribers.

[57] CMS administers the Medicare program as well as oversees the design and operation of state Medicaid programs. To receive federal matching funds for services provided to Medicaid beneficiaries, each state must submit a state Medicaid plan for approval by CMS. The state Medicaid plan defines how the state will operate its Medicaid program, including which populations and services are covered. States must operate their Medicaid programs within broad federal parameters. While complying with these federal requirements, however, states have the flexibility to tailor their Medicaid programs.

[58] GAO/AIMD-00-21.3.1.

End Notes for Appendix I

[1] The states vetted were: Arizona, California, Florida, Illinois, Maryland, Michigan, New Jersey, New York, Ohio, Pennsylvania, and Texas.

[2] Mathematica Policy Research, Inc., *MSIS State Data Characteristics/Anomalies Report* (Jan. 7, 2013).

[3] Department of Health and Human Services, Office of Inspector General, *Early Assessment of Review of Medicaid Integrity Contractors*, OEI-05-10-00200 (Washington, D.C.: February 2012); GAO, *National Medicaid Audit Program: CMS Should Improve Reporting and Focus on Audit Collaboration with States*, GAO-12-627 (Washington, D.C.: June 14, 2012); and *Medicaid: Data Sets Provide Inconsistent Picture of Expenditures*, GAO-13-47 (Washington, D.C.: Nov. 29, 2012).

[4] Mathematica Policy Research serves as CMS's contractor and performs reviews to ensure and report on the quality of MSIS data. The organization publishes information on unreconciled data in its anomalies report.

[5] Under managed-care arrangements, states contract with MCOs to deliver care through networks. States typically pay the MCOs a fixed amount each month, called a capitation payment. Approximately 70 percent of Medicaid enrollees are served through managed-care delivery systems, where providers are paid at a monthly capitation payment rate.

[6] Drugs and other substances that are considered controlled substances under the Controlled Substances Act are divided into five schedules. An updated and complete list of the schedules is published annually in 21 C.F.R. §§ 1308.11 – 1308.15. Substances are placed in their respective schedules based on whether they have a currently accepted medical use in treatment in the United States, their relative abuse potential, and likelihood of causing dependence when abused. Drugs that are not considered controlled substances are known as noncontrolled substances.

[7] Our analysis did not control for medications where there was not a generic version available.

[8] When a change to a prescription is made or when a beneficiary fails to pick up the prescribed drugs, the pharmacy must adjust the claim transaction. According to officials in New Jersey, instances of pharmacies with too many or too few adjustments may be red flags for concern.

[9] Our review did not include all drugs that may be used to treat HIV or diabetes.

[10] This analysis was based on diagnosis codes for HIV or diabetes. We did not account for prescribing of these medications for other ailments.

[11] GAO, *Standards for Internal Control in the Federal Government*, GAO/AIMD-00-21.3.1 (Washington, D.C.: November 1999).

[12] GAO, *Individual Disaster Assistance Programs: Framework for Fraud Prevention, Detection, and Prosecution*, GAO-06-954T (Washington, D.C.: July 12, 2006).

INDEX

A

abuse, vii, 1, 2, 5, 6, 15, 25, 31, 35, 41, 42, 43, 44, 45, 46, 47, 51, 52, 54, 56, 57, 62, 63, 66, 67, 68, 72, 73, 74, 79, 81, 82, 83
access, 3, 13, 20, 26, 27, 28, 29, 31
adjustment, 57, 65
administrators, 46, 47, 74
age, 8, 29, 34, 54, 70
agencies, 9, 15, 20, 22, 26, 29, 36, 37, 70
Appropriations Committee, 53
audit(s), 7, 9, 35, 46, 48, 52, 65, 66, 67, 72, 73, 78
authorities, 13
average costs, 65

B

benefits, 2, 3, 5, 7, 8, 10, 11, 12, 13, 14, 19, 20, 27, 29, 34, 37, 47, 48, 53, 61, 62, 77, 78, 82

C

care model, 36
category a, 66
challenges, 38, 53
chemicals, 82
China, 14
citizenship, 8, 16, 20
classes, 47, 55, 75, 81
cocaine, 83
Code of Federal Regulations, 36
coding, 71, 81
commercial, 33
community, 49
compliance, 65, 67
computer, 37
confidentiality, 37
consumers, 8
controlled substances, 43, 45, 65, 66, 79, 81, 83
Controlled Substances Act, 79, 83
coordination, 37
cost, 6, 13, 14, 42, 43, 54, 55, 58, 59, 61, 62, 63, 65, 67, 68, 81
cost saving, 63, 68, 69
credentials, 23
current limit, 13

D

data analysis, 29, 58, 59, 60, 65, 71, 81
data availability, 80
data collection, 50, 70
data set, 53
database, 3, 26, 27, 28, 30, 31, 34, 35, 38, 50, 77
deaths, 20, 23

deficiencies, 52
Department of Defense, 37
Department of Health and Human Services, 4, 13, 22, 34, 38, 44, 61, 73, 77, 79, 83
Department of Homeland Security, 16
depth, 69, 71
detection, 65, 82
diabetes, 47, 57, 59, 60, 71, 75, 79, 81, 83, 84
directors, 51, 52
disbursement, 4
disclosure, 37
District of Columbia, 36
diversity, 38, 46, 73
DMF, 3, 6, 10, 11, 14, 19, 20, 23, 28, 29, 33, 36, 38, 44
doctors, 42, 45
dosage, 83
draft, 20, 28, 29, 38, 69, 71, 72, 80
Drug Enforcement Administration, 23, 65
drug interaction, 64
drug trafficking, 15
drug treatment, 58
drugs, 43, 45, 46, 47, 49, 50, 54, 55, 56, 57, 61, 62, 64, 65, 66, 73, 74, 75, 79, 80, 81, 82, 83

E

eligibility criteria, 8
e-mail, 28, 70
emergency, 80
enforcement, 8, 9
enrollment, 1, 2, 3, 5, 6, 8, 11, 13, 15, 16, 19, 20, 25, 26, 27, 28, 30, 31, 36, 38, 46, 49, 73
environment, 24
evidence, 7, 35, 48, 57, 71, 75, 78
exclusion, 6, 8, 15, 34, 48, 77
expenditures, 5, 7, 9, 41, 46, 69, 74
exposure, 63
extracts, 26, 34, 77

F

federal government, vii, 1, 2, 4, 6, 7, 9, 14, 16, 27, 34, 36, 39, 41, 44, 48, 49, 62, 68, 77, 79, 84
federal law, 8, 30, 42, 44, 63
federal regulations, 8, 10, 16, 26
financial, 16, 80
fiscal year, vii, 1, 2, 4, 5, 9, 12, 13, 14, 15, 16, 19, 20, 27, 29, 30, 31, 32, 33, 34, 37, 38, 41, 42, 44, 46, 47, 51, 52, 54, 57, 58, 59, 60, 61, 62, 63, 66, 68, 70, 71, 74, 75, 76, 77, 80, 82
flexibility, 7, 8, 49, 83
Food and Drug Administration, 58, 76, 81
funds, 4, 11, 30, 33, 37, 44, 45, 61, 66, 68, 76, 83

G

GAO, 1, 2, 3, 7, 10, 13, 18, 22, 35, 36, 38, 39, 41, 42, 43, 46, 47, 48, 52, 55, 58, 60, 61, 73, 75, 78, 79, 80, 81, 83, 84
General Services Administration (GSA), 4, 6, 13, 34, 44, 48, 61, 77
generic drugs, 56, 64
government funds, 68
governments, 35, 78
GSA, 4, 15, 34, 37, 44, 62, 65, 77, 82
Guam, 36
guidance, 2, 3, 9, 14, 15, 19, 24, 25, 27, 28, 35, 36, 42, 43, 44, 51, 52, 63, 66, 67, 68, 69, 72, 78
guidelines, 4, 49

H

health, 2, 4, 7, 8, 9, 11, 13, 14, 16, 23, 25, 43, 44, 45, 47, 49, 50, 51, 61, 62, 64, 74, 82
health care, 7, 15, 44, 62
HHS, 4, 6, 9, 13, 15, 19, 20, 22, 23, 24, 25, 28, 34, 44, 46, 48, 50, 52, 53, 57, 61, 62, 65, 69, 70, 73, 77, 80, 81

history, 66, 75
HIV, 44, 47, 50, 57, 58, 59, 71, 75, 79, 80, 81, 83, 84
House of Representatives, 4
household composition, 8, 11
household income, 11, 16
hub, 2, 4, 16, 19, 20, 37
human, 43, 44, 47, 75
human immunodeficiency virus, 43, 44, 47, 75

I

identification, 5, 31, 32, 55
identity, 6, 11, 12, 33, 34, 48, 62, 76, 77
immigration, 3, 8, 16
improvements, 15, 68
incarceration, 3, 11, 15, 16, 20, 30, 32, 62, 71, 76
incidence, 10
income, 4, 7, 8, 44
India, 14
individuals, 3, 4, 5, 6, 7, 8, 11, 14, 15, 19, 20, 24, 27, 30, 32, 33, 34, 35, 36, 37, 44, 45, 47, 61, 62, 66, 71, 75, 76, 77, 81, 82
infrastructure, 52
inmates, 11, 61
institutions, 11, 14, 61
integration, 36
integrity, 1, 2, 3, 5, 6, 9, 24, 25, 31, 35, 36, 41, 42, 44, 45, 48, 50, 62, 64, 69, 78
internal controls, 68, 72
International Classification of Diseases, 76
Israel, 37
issues, 16, 20, 30, 31, 38, 46, 51, 64, 70, 71, 74, 81

L

labeling, 58, 76
laws, 5, 9, 35, 44, 50, 78
laws and regulations, 50
legislation, 49
local authorities, 11, 62

M

majority, 51, 57, 59
management, 11, 14, 30, 33, 36, 50, 72
Maryland, 38, 51, 70, 79, 80, 83
median, 57, 81
medical, 7, 11, 13, 31, 37, 45, 49, 56, 57, 58, 60, 61, 65, 67, 70, 73, 74, 78, 79, 80, 82, 83
medical history, 57, 58, 60
medical reason, 56, 80
Medicare, vii, 2, 3, 4, 10, 13, 15, 18, 22, 24, 25, 26, 27, 28, 31, 36, 42, 43, 44, 45, 50, 52, 61, 62, 67, 68, 73, 79, 80, 83
medication, 42, 47, 54, 57, 58, 64, 67, 70, 71, 75, 81
medicine, 24
membership, 23
methadone, 83
methamphetamine, 83
methodology, 7, 28, 49, 69
Mexico, 37
military, 33
milligrams, 83
money laundering, 15
murder, 15

N

needy, 4, 44
neglect, 2, 15, 62
nursing, 49, 57
nursing care, 57

O

Office of Management and Budget, 36
Office of the Inspector General, 73
officials, 2, 6, 7, 8, 11, 15, 19, 20, 23, 24, 26, 27, 35, 37, 38, 42, 46, 47, 48, 51, 52, 53, 56, 59, 62, 66, 67, 68, 70, 74, 78, 79, 80, 81, 82, 83
operations, 63, 68
opportunities, 15

outpatient, 45, 47, 54, 57, 58, 59, 71, 75
oversight, 2, 4, 6, 9, 25, 29, 35, 42, 43, 45, 48, 50, 53, 59, 63, 70, 71, 72, 73, 78, 82
ownership, 3, 8, 26, 27, 28

P

participants, 37
permit, 65
pharmaceuticals, 48, 78
Philippines, 37
physicians, 8, 13, 22, 36, 81
platform, 53
policy, 35, 50, 67, 68, 78
population, 8, 26, 30, 51, 53, 65, 67, 71, 76
population group, 8
prescription drugs, 42, 45, 46, 47, 48, 49, 57, 62, 72, 73, 74, 76, 80, 82
prevention, 25, 49, 68, 82
prisons, 15, 62
procurement, 15
professionals, 8, 22
profit, 55
program administration, 35, 36, 78
project, 53

R

racketeering, 15
real-time basis, 71
recommendations, 2, 28, 29, 31, 45, 72, 73
recreational, 80
regulations, 3, 6, 7, 16, 18, 19, 22, 23, 25, 35, 37, 44, 48, 49, 65, 66, 67, 78
regulatory requirements, 9
reimburse, 49
reliability, 7, 29, 30, 35, 45, 48, 51, 70, 73, 78, 80
requirement(s), 7, 8, 9, 11, 9, 23, 24, 25, 26, 30, 36, 37, 43, 49, 53, 78, 79, 82, 83, 137,
resources, 16, 19, 67
respiratory medications, 42, 47, 55, 66, 75, 81

response, 16, 28, 29, 35, 38, 71, 72, 78, 80
restrictions, 63, 82
retail, 67, 71, 72
risk, 5, 8, 23, 24, 26, 32, 36, 38, 44, 47, 56, 64, 66, 68, 74, 78, 81
routes, 16
rules, 65

S

safety, 42, 63, 64, 68
sanctions, 13
Saudi Arabia, 14
savings, 63, 68
scope, 7, 29, 49, 51, 70, 82
services, 3, 5, 6, 7, 8, 10, 11, 13, 14, 19, 22, 31, 32, 34, 37, 38, 46, 47, 48, 49, 50, 54, 61, 62, 67, 70, 72, 74, 75, 77, 78, 81, 82, 83
Social Security, 3, 4, 6, 7, 10, 13, 32, 36, 38, 44, 48, 61, 76
Social Security Administration, 3, 4, 6, 10, 13, 32, 44, 48, 61, 76
society, 23
specialists, 56
spending, 64, 70
SSA, 4, 6, 10, 11, 12, 13, 14, 16, 20, 23, 27, 28, 29, 30, 32, 36, 38, 44, 48, 61, 65, 69, 76
stakeholders, 51
standardization, 25
state oversight, vii, 1, 5, 6, 31, 35, 41, 45, 48, 57, 59, 73, 78
statistics, 20, 65
statutes, 6, 7, 35, 37, 48, 49, 78
stock, 67
stockpiling, 43, 67, 72
substance abuse, 70
substitution, 56
Supplemental Nutrition Assistance Program, 37
suppliers, 3, 23

T

tactics, 65
target, 57
tax evasion, 2, 15
technical assistance, 4, 9, 28, 44, 49
technical comments, 28, 70
testing, 7, 35, 38, 46, 48, 73, 78
theft, 2, 11, 12, 15, 62, 82
time frame, 29, 79, 80
training, 9
transactions, 51, 52, 54
transplant recipients, 81
treatment, 24, 75, 79, 82, 83

U

United States, v, 1, 4, 6, 13, 14, 33, 41, 53, 62, 79, 82, 83

V

validation, 25, 52

W

waiver, 8
Washington, 36, 38, 39, 79, 80, 83, 84
waste, 5, 25, 43, 44, 45, 47, 50, 51, 52, 54, 56, 57, 63, 67, 68, 72, 74, 81, 82